Readers Theatre Comes to Church

Gordon C. Bennett

 JOHN KNOX PRESS
Richmond, Virginia

ACKNOWLEDGMENTS

My thanks are due the various authors and publishers who have permitted portions of their work to be included here, either as supporting quotations or illustrative material in the text, or as sample reading scripts.

Many people have directly or indirectly enabled me to get to the point of writing such a book—it is impossible to fully acknowledge this assistance. I think now of three individuals who have been especially helpful. One was Mildred Hahn Enterline, whose contagious love of drama hooked me when I worked under her direction at the American Baptist Assembly, Green Lake, Wisconsin, and who turned me on to drama as potent Christian expression. Another was Charles Laughton, whose tour of the college circuit included Dickinson College in my under-graduate days there, and whose artistry on the reading platform inspired and awakened me to the strength of oral interpretation at its magnificent best. Thirdly, I want to recognize Professor Melvin R. White, now of California, whose writings and personal correspondence on Readers Theatre have considerably broadened my mind.

Various others—students, teachers, authors, family, friends—have assisted me in little or large ways in this task. Most of them don't even know how they've helped. They are unnamed but not forgotten.

Gordon C. Bennett

Scripture quotations are from the *Revised Standard Version of the Bible*, copyrighted 1946 and 1952 by the Division of Christian Education of the National Council of Churches

Excerpts from *Readers Theatre Handbook* by Coger and White, copyright © 1967 by Scott, Foresman and Company, are reprinted by permission.

Library of Congress Cataloging in Publication Data

Bennett, Gordon C
    Readers theatre comes to church.

    Bibliography: p.
    1. Oral interpretation. 2. Religious drama—
Presentation, etc. I. Title.
PN4145.B43   792½.022   72–1763
ISBN 0–8042–1963–X

Dramatic Expression in the Church

Our assistant minister was ecstatic a week later. "I've had lots of compliments about that service!" he told me, and he sounded as though he was referring to more genuine feedback than the usual "Nice sermon today, Reverend" at the door following a worship service.

That Thanksgiving Sunday sermon had not raised many eyebrows, for this congregation is used to strange happenings. But it did seem to hold the audience's attention and stretch their minds. We had decided to integrate portions of scene one of Archibald MacLeish's *J.B.* with some commentary by the assistant pastor, and that would be the sermon for the day. So a reading team of five presented three brief passages from the play interspersed with interpretive comments by the preacher. The basic theme was timely and appropriate—J.B.'s insistence that the affluence and prosperity represented by the Turkey Day feast was not something that could be earned but was a free gift of God. In one sense, the dialogues read from the play were sermon illustrations; in another sense, the preacher's commentary was an exegesis of the drama. Certainly it was lively communication, and a Christian message was preached through the combination of media.

This was one successful use of Readers Theatre. I have worked with it on many other occasions—in church, on the college campus, at youth conferences and retreat centers. I find it very exciting! This book is a manual for anybody with a dramatic interest who likes to read aloud or enjoys being read to—and especially for Christians interested in innovative means of expression. It's a manual for pastors, directors of Christian education, amateur thespians, young people. It doesn't matter that you've not had any dramatic experience. This book will show you some ways to use Readers Theatre. If the book does no more than turn you on to the use of informal drama in the church, it has been worth publishing.

Does the book's title seem pretentious? Frankly, it is. It's wishful thinking. Readers Theatre is not being used all that much in the church today. Many creative people are using it; more will use it. But lots of good Christians never consider using dramatic forms to present Christian truth. That's their loss. A fascinating medium with huge potential for Christian communication is left unexplored by those people.

And for some, there's still that old hang-up about "theatre." Putting the word "theatre" into the same sentence with "church" may be a problem for some—but you're past that point, right? If not, let me point out that in the Greek, *theatre* means "a seeing-place," and surely the church is a place where eyes are opened. That's what the gospel is about. And the Puritan objection that acting is deceitful because you're pretending to be something you're not just won't wash in Readers Theatre where people don't act but read! (Ah, but how they read!)

Whatever form it takes, theatre in the church can be explosively incarnational. The church becomes a stage for the demonstration of God's action and the faith-response of his people. Those who watch and listen are provoked to encounter him and live out his gifts of love and hope in their lives. So the church becomes a theatre of exultation and of arousal, both of which are needed in this day of despair and indifference. Readers Theatre can meet this need economically—it may be the most pliable and viable form of dramatic expression for the church.

Contents

Readers Theatre Comes to Church

PRINCIPLES AND PROCEDURES

Readers Theatre:
Descriptions and Definitions

For two and a half hours the audience seemed to be unaware that they were not seeing a full performance of *Lost in the Stars*. They were too completely absorbed in the suffering of Kumalo to notice that the actor portraying the role was holding a script. The sought-after moment of "dramatic involvement" was vibrant in the church hall. Maxwell Anderson's adaptation of Alan Paton's *Cry, the Beloved Country* communicated the power of universal suffering, of the question of sin, and of one man's Christlike compassion toward his fellow man. The fact that the audience was watching a group of actors in street clothes reading scripts before a neutral background did not really impress them one way or another. The thoughts and feelings of the characters were penetrating the actors' voices and bodies, and the illusion of dramatic truth was realized.

When the last act was over and Kurt Weill's music was lost in space, the silence that gripped the church group was evidence that something had happened and was happening in their inner consciousness. Thoughts were changing, realizations were taking place, motivations were being transformed. The important factor was not the lack of something outward, but the power of something inward. And that is just the power of informal drama.[1]

What James Warren described in 1961 as "informal drama" is today identified usually as *Readers Theatre*, although other labels—such as concert reading, interpreter's theatre—have been applied to it. Readers Theatre is increasingly being used on college and university campuses as either a supplement to or a substitute for the conventional theatre program. Perhaps one-fifth of all theatrical productions at large American universities are done as Readers Theatre. Also, this medium is being used more now on the secondary school level as well as among civic and club groups and in churches.

Professionally, Readers Theatre made its important debut in 1951 with the famous quartet of Charles Boyer, Sir Cedric Hardwicke, Charles Laughton, and Agnes Moorehead presenting *Don Juan in Hell* to appreciative audiences. This, the third act of Shaw's *Man and Superman*, was read from scripts placed on lecterns with the interpreters seated on stools. The immense success of *Don Juan in Hell* gave impetus to later professional readings of *John Brown's Body, Brecht on Brecht, Spoon River Anthology, Under Milk Wood, The World of Carl Sandburg,* and others. In the late sixties, *In White America,* a documentary play depicting American racism, was read to profoundly disturbed audiences across the country. These professional events have stimulated the amateur growth of Readers Theatre on campuses and in communities from Alaska to Florida. So much for its growing popularity. Just what is Readers Theatre?

Toward a Useful Definition

First, you will notice that I haven't placed an apostrophe after the *s* in our title *Readers Theatre.* This is deliberate. *Readers' Theatre* would imply that it is theatre *of* and *for* readers. It is that—but much more than that! Two other elements are involved: the audience, to whom something is read, and the literature, from which ideas and emotion are conveyed. The theatre does not belong to the readers, as the apostrophe would imply, but to all three parties in combination.

Now, Readers Theatre cannot be defined *exactly.* It is not the same as conventional theatre in which lines are memorized and acted out within a certain setting. Nor is it simply reading aloud, although it does involve group reading. Perhaps it is a compromise between oral interpretation of literature and conventional theatre, but in some ways it is distinct from both. Perhaps the best definition is the simplest: *Readers Theatre is the oral interpretation of literature by a group of readers for an audience.* Armstrong and Brandes put it like this:

> The staged reading, as its name implies, is a compromise between drama and oral interpretation, in which readers adopt a limited amount of the technique of the theatre without making any pretense of "giving a play."[2]

Keith Brooks of Ohio State University gives this description:

> Readers Theatre is a group activity in which the best of literature is communicated from manuscript to an audience through the oral communication approach of vocal and physical suggestion.[3]

And Wallace Bacon of Northwestern University has written:

> Readers Theatre, in our discussion, embraces the group reading of material involving delineated characters, with or without the presence of a narrator, in such a manner as to establish the locus of the piece not onstage with the readers but in the imagination of the audience.[4]

These definitions imply a distinction between Readers Theatre and the choral readings that have often found their way into both church and theatre. Speech choirs, from the days of the fifth-century Greek chorus onward, have tried to communicate ideas in some sort of group vocal harmony or in unison, from poetic materials such as Homer, Sophocles, or the Bible. But Readers Theatre is not particularly interested in *unison* reading and it is not limited to *poetic* materials. It does share ideas from literature, but through the impersonation of characters it tries to project an invisible scene or scenes into the listeners' imaginations. Readers Theatre uses narrative, expository, satirical, and dramatic materials—not just poetry—and it may employ some theatrical devices which a speech choir would never consider. Choral speaking is an effective way to present poetic or Biblical materials, but Readers Theatre is more exciting than the speech choir approach; it is more versatile and dramatically more powerful.

Let's compare the two forms in terms of doing a presentation of Scripture. Suppose you take one of Jesus' parables, such as the story of the rich man and Lazarus, and break it down into lines for solo readers, light and dark voices, and unison reading—you have a speech choir manuscript. Suppose that instead you break the passage into narration and dialogue, giving different readers particular characters to interpret and training them to project the scene psychologically into the audience—you have Readers Theatre. Either form can be effective but Readers Theatre may be the more effective medium where dialogue, scene, and dramatic action are basic to the literature.

Readers Theatre and Theatre

So Readers Theatre is not the same as choral speech; neither is it the same as conventional theatre. Students of the art have long argued the question of where oral interpretation leaves off and acting begins. We often say that the better actors effectively "interpret" their lines; also it is obvious that the best readers possess dramatic instinct. The difference between the interpreter and the actor may hinge on two factors—the degree of impersonation and the focus of attention. The actor assumes a role and tries to identify very strongly with his character; to a large extent, he *becomes* the character. The oral interpreter, although he achieves a limited identification, does not become the character he is reading, but he *suggests* the character. This makes it possible for him to read various characters in a particular piece without so much as changing position onstage.

The other difference lies in the focus of attention. The actor, along with his colleagues, focuses attention upon their scene on stage; the actors look at each other, *establishing a visible reality onstage.* The oral interpreter, who may or may not look at his fellow readers, focuses attention on the ideas and the imaginary characters in the literature, *projecting an invisible reality into his listeners' minds.*

Readers Theatre has aptly been described as "theatre of the mind" by Leslie Irene Coger and Melvin R. White, who have written the most useful handbook on the subject.[5] The readers' function is to present the material in such a way that it will evoke powerful images in their auditors' minds. These images will congeal into a scene, subjectively real as the listener conjures up related experiences, attitudes, and ideas. So we have a theatre of imagination, a theatre which demands more psychological involvement on the part of listeners than does conventional theatre. Usually Readers Theatre is performed on a bare stage, so the listener must conjure up scenery, the characters and their appearance, and the various physical actions *in his mind's eye.* Because it requires so much of his imagination, the listener may become much more vicariously involved than in conventional theatre. That is, provided it is worth the effort to him! Frankly, some audiences, particularly the ignorant or those to whom Readers Theatre is very strange—those who have had a steady diet of movies or television—may turn off instead of turn on! But over a period of time, and with some education as to the purpose and the dynamic of Readers Theatre, their attitudes may change. Many people can testify to the impact of this medium in their experience.

So Readers Theatre is not stage-centered but audience-centered; it is not actor-centered but idea-centered. So . . .

> A Readers Theatre presentation differs from a conventional play in that it demands stricter attention to the aural elements of the literature. The interpreter must express the emotions, the attitudes, and the actions of the characters by economically using his face, his voice, and his body as vocal and physical clues to meaning. Nothing he does should distract the audience's attention from the characters, the scene, and the action within the literature.[6]

Wallace Bacon graphically describes the difference between conventional and Readers Theatre:

> Perhaps we may put it this way: A blind man has less to lose in attending a performance in Readers Theatre than in attending a performance in conventional theatre. *This is not to say that he will lose nothing.* A deaf man has less to lose in attending a performance in conventional theatre than in attending a performance in Readers Theatre. *This is not to say that he will lose nothing.*[7]

Some Background

Although the history of oral interpretation is ancient—as storytelling it may predate any other form of dramatic expression—Readers Theatre as we know it is essentially a modern invention. There are hints of it in the recitations of the *rhapsodes*—itinerant storytellers of ancient Greece[8] —but their renderings of Homer were usually solo performances. There are suggestions of it in the role of the chorus in the Greek theatre, and in the dialogue that developed within the Lenten liturgy of the medieval church, but definite evidence of the Readers Theatre approach is lacking. Since the Renaissance we have a few accounts of play-reading clubs or groups, such as this description of a London club about 1806:

> Another species of dramatic reading has of late years been practised in private companies assemblied for that purpose . . . In this entertainment, as on the stage, the characters of the drama are distributed among the readers according to their supposed talents; and each being furnished with a separate book, either the whole play, or certain select scenes from one or more, are read by the performers sitting around a table, whilst others of the company serve as the audience.[9]

So although it has a few antecedents, Readers Theatre has blossomed in the twentieth century. It has come into prominence since World War II, in fact. It's partially a reaction against the naturalistic stage which tried to represent reality as a "slice of life," with its peculiar fourth-wall convention that pretends that the audience is peeking in on something it is not supposed to see. Realism—more properly, naturalism—has dominated Western theatre since Ibsen.

Many modern playwrights, however, have tried to return the theatre to that presentational style which was common to most of its history; from ancient Greece through Shakespeare dramatists had recognized the audience and had played to it directly, using narrators, asides, soliloquies, circular seating, the thrust stage, etc. Prior to World War II Thornton Wilder pioneered the revival of presentational theatre with his marvelous *Our Town*, a captivatingly warm study of life in a New England village. Presented first in 1938, this play made extensive use of a narrator-stage manager who addressed the audience, and the action was played with fragments of scenery on a bare stage against a neutral backdrop. Wilder wanted to stimulate his spectators' imaginations and catch them up in the experience fully—the time and sweep of eternity revealed in *Our Town*.

The German playwright Bertolt Brecht dominated eastern European theatre in the first half of this century with his "epic" approach. Brecht's concern was that the audience is so emotionally involved in most drama that it loses all objectivity. He wanted his audiences to maintain a certain detachment so that they could think, evaluate, and draw lessons from the material presented on stage. Brecht introduced certain "alienating devices" meant to keep the audience at a safe emotional distance, reminding them that, after all, they were watching a play and not life itself. These devices, similar to many Readers Theatre techniques, included the use of a narrator, role changes by the actors during the play, asides and songs sung out of character, and visual images or messages projected on screens over the stage. Although Readers Theatre cannot and will not keep the audience emotionally detached, its methods are in many respects similar to those of Brecht. Like the work of Brecht, Wilder, and many others, its approach is frankly presentational. Readers Theatre may be another attempt to break free of the confining cage in which the conventions of the naturalistic stage have put modern drama.

Using It in the Church

Many church groups use play readings to provoke thought or to stimulate discussion; this is hardly new. A church school class or study group may read a play or a scene from a play and then talk about it. This may be enlightening. Technically, it wouldn't be Readers Theatre until the group presented that reading to an audience larger than itself—say the Sunday evening congregation or another church group across town. But let's not quibble—even if it's read by a small class for its own edification I'd call it Readers Theatre if it conforms to our previous definitions.

Often youth groups read plays or dialogues for discussion purposes at their meetings. One of many resources for this use is Ann Billups' *Discussion Starters for Youth Groups*,[10] which is not sterling drama but does accomplish its purpose—these are lively, brief dialogue-skits which stimulate thinking on various issues related to faith and morality. Also, Friendship Press has published a number of discussion-starter plays meant to be read in classes, workshops, or seminars on evangelism, missions, or the Christian life (see Bibliography).

Certainly the educational values of play readings plus discussion are clear. Of course, some dramatic material is not discussable—it may have a very pointed conclusion that everyone accepts or it may end on a sober note that lends itself to silent reflection rather than talk. But provocative material can be selected that is open-ended or, if not open-ended, that will at least arouse disagreement or provoke thought about its application to life. The leader of such a session could print discussion guides for use following the reading or could list starter questions on chalkboard or newsprint. Or, before the reading, the leader might ask the audience to look for certain things or be prepared to answer certain questions. An interesting device is to stop the reading midway or just prior to the denouement and ask, "How do you feel now?" or "Where do you think this is going?" or "What's the solution to this problem?" and then continue with the reading after the listeners react. Of course, some readings could not be broken in this way; discretion is needed.

Any group in the church might develop a reading team for its own benefit or for the benefit of the entire congregation. An adult class which has read *A Man for All Seasons* may volunteer to present a cutting at a midweek service. A youth group which has studied Shaw's trial scene in *Saint Joan* may want to present it to an ecumenical gathering of young people. A study group reading Lenten drama may offer a reading of *The Terrible Meek* or *Christ in the Concrete City* during a Lenten service or preceding Holy Communion on Maundy Thursday. The committee charged with the annual Christmas play may decide to read R. H. Ward's verse drama *The Holy Family* (or, if the occasion is gay and festive, Charles Dickens' *A Christmas Carol*). The occasions for Readers Theatre in church life are many indeed.

What about worship? If you're open to innovative forms, Readers Theatre can become a vital part of your worship experiences. Increasingly we're becoming aware of the relationship between worship and drama. You can find lots of dramatic elements in worship, such as *dialogue* (between man and God in prayer, through the proclamation of God's Word, etc.), some kind of *conflict* (between God and the forces of evil, between man and his lower nature, between the church and its opponents in the world, etc.), and the development of an *action* leading to a *climax* (a high moment of inspiration, a time of personal commitment, the sending forth of apostles, etc.). Furthermore, in some rituals of the church—like baptism or the Lord's Supper—we have a dramatic experience reenacted over and over. Obviously there's an affinity between worship and drama. Not everybody is conscious of it, but many are; for many people an inspirational drama can itself be a means of grace, an act of faith, or a moment of worship. This can happen if the dramatic piece is carefully chosen for its religious significance and if the actors or readers present it as an offering to God, forgetting themselves. (That's hard but it's possible.)

Ronald Sleeth speaks of the gospel as the "Great Dramatic Event" and suggests that the preacher's task is to "reveal it in the most persuasive way." As he puts it, "The basic principle of dramatization is to place truth in such imaginative form that people respond through several of their senses."[11] If the preacher's task is to dramatize truth, it seems logical that a form that is inherently dramatic will help him. Readers Theatre may well become a mainstay of Sunday worship. You may want to develop a permanent reading team to assist your pastor with worship—using scenes, cuttings, or scripts that would relate to various themes used in worship and that would supplement the sermon. In fact, if the idea catches on, you may find that occasionally you are asked to replace the sermon—no doubt to the relief of many pew-sitters!

In Central Baptist Church of Wayne, Pennsylvania, where I hold membership, we have used a lot of Readers Theatre in worship—specifically, on fourteen occasions during the past year. Sometimes the material is better suited to the contemporary worship service held at the early hour, with seating arena-style in the fellowship hall; on other occasions it's performed in the more traditional sanctuary service at the late hour. We have to be slightly more careful in selecting material for the latter, since some of the people who attend at 11:15 are very conservative.

On one Sunday, for example, two of us read the parts of the King and Thomas Becket from the scene on the beach in Anouilh's play where the exiled Becket, returning from France, makes his stirring defense of "the honor of God." (The pastor enlarged on that phrase in his meditation.) On a Sunday morning in June, with the service geared to the topic of marriage, a group did a lively reading of the wedding scene in *Our Town*, replete with a few appropriate bars of music by the pianist. At another time, with the pastor talking about the Christian's duty toward ecology, four people read a cutting from the old but very timely drama *An Enemy of the People*, by Ibsen. We have had an element in the order of service for the sanctuary hour titled "The Bible in Life," and several times we did our reading in that time slot of about five minutes, with the theme of the reading often related to the themes of the Scripture passage and the sermon.

Some very creative things have happened at our early service, in which innovation is the rule. On one occasion, when the pastor wanted to dedicate some babies (keep in mind that we are speaking of a Baptist church!), he developed the entire experience around the ideas of birth, creation, and life. The congregation gathered, arena-style, around a rug on which the infants played at the center of worship. Besides the brief ritual of dedication, worship consisted of appropriate folk songs and spirituals, Scripture, relevant poetry (by Kahlil Gibran), special music, film clips from a film on natural childbirth, a dramatic reading, a brief sermon, and the benediction. For the benediction, children were given balloons to blow up, and they were released on signal to rocket throughout the room accompanied by shouts of glee—as sign of the freedom and joy of new life. The dramatic reading, which I invented for the occasion, was an important element: a simple dialogue between a dispatching angel in Heaven and a rather impatient unborn soul named Jimmy, in a waiting room prior to Jimmy's arrival on earth. Jimmy is very upset about going to that "backward planet" until the angel explains that he is being sent only because he is "full of hope and promise." At the pastor's request, the reading was repeated at a similar service later. So keep in mind that a creative worship experience may require created material—you don't have to stay with the classics! Your congregation may include professional writers or idea people who have the talent to develop dramatic readings for worship.

If this is new to your congregation, it may be necessary to introduce the reading rather carefully as it is made part of worship. Naturally, it helps if the pastor refers to it during his sermon, but it may also be necessary to add transitional comments to bridge the gaps between the reading and other parts of the service. If your readings are obviously related to your worship themes, after the congregation has heard several such readings, you may not have to explain yourself anymore as to the purpose and function of the reading. By then your people probably welcome the Readers Theatre bits as an aid to worship and another perspective on the theme.

In preparing this book, I sent questionnaires about this medium to a hundred ministers and directors of Christian education in Presbyterian and Baptist churches in America. While fewer than half responded, many showed a real understanding of and appreciation for Readers Theatre. The following list of projects culled from these questionnaire replies shows the extent and variety of uses for Readers Theatre in the church.

One church did Stephen Vincent Benét's *A Child Is Born* for a Christmas program; another read a Christmas play, Tubbs' *Holiday House.*

Cuttings from Arthur Miller's *Death of a Salesman* were used in two different study groups on the subject "The Nature of Man."

One church did *The Terrible Meek,* by Charles Rann Kennedy, as a reading in a worship experience planned by the youth; another youth group presented a brief segment of Dorothy Sayers' radio drama *The Man Born to Be King* as a climax to a Sunday morning service.

Cuttings from T. S. Eliot were read and discussed in a play-reading group.

A portion of Shakespeare's *Othello* was read at a program for the congregation of one church, demonstrating the great damage caused by jealousy; four readers sat around a table in the church chapel.

Philip William Turner's impressive choral drama on the passion of Christ, *Christ in the Concrete City,* was done as a reading program. Another Lenten reading, *Behold the Man,* a series of dialogues by Paul Keller and Stan Kloth on the question of the Christian as peacemaker, was read in three services during Holy Week.

Another church reported using Oscar Rumpf's choric reading *Standing Room Only* as part of worship. Mr. Rumpf has a number of contemporary choric readings which, although they are not Readers Theatre if it requires delineated characters, provide extremely stimulating input for worship.[12] Many church groups have used them successfully because of their timeliness and spiritual relevance.

A church with a capable reading team might eventually present its material to other churches or to denominational or ecumenical conventions and assemblies. But keep in mind that you don't have to go it alone; if your church seems to lack the personnel for this, talk with other churches in your community and develop an ecumenical Readers Theatre troupe! Also remember that Readers Theatre doesn't require a huge number of voices; one interpreter can read several parts, so a team of five can develop a rather wide repertory.

I haven't explored the possibilities of Readers Theatre for evangelism; maybe you will! Outside of the church proper you will find the courtyard, the village square, the shopping center, the community park. Maybe these are places where Readers Theatre, among other dramatic methods, will prove itself useful as a means of presenting Christian material to a secular society.

The possibilities of Readers Theatre for worship, teaching, and evangelism are limited only by the boundaries of the imaginations of Christian people.

Summing Up

Readers Theatre as we know it is still very experimental, so I just can't be highly definitive. But, in general, these are the characteristics of the medium:

1. In Readers Theatre we stress the meanings in the literature, which are conveyed through the vocal-physical skills of a group of interpreters.

2. Reading manuscripts are carried and openly displayed.

3. Physical movement is limited and suggestive in nature.

4. The interpreters project an imaginary scene into the minds of their audience. Often they use offstage focus to do this (which will be explained later).

5. Usually there are delineated characters and a story line, and a reader may interpret more than one character.

6. Generally, a bare platform is used for the reading, with scenery or technical effects used sparingly or not at all.

7. Narration quite often is used to establish scenes, make transitions, fix the mood, provide exposition; often one or more readers become the narrator.

James Warren says that two words indicate the basic principle of informal drama: *simplicity* and *imagination*.[13] Conventional theatre by its use of spectacle often distracts the spectator from the ideas or meanings presented. Readers Theatre in its simplicity strips away the nonessentials and makes people listen to the lines, imagine the rest, and get the meanings. Its many advantages can be condensed into these statements:

1. Readers Theatre makes use of a variety of material, including essays, novels, stories, and poetry, as well as plays.

2. It eliminates the need for memorization of lines verbatim, which eliminates much of the stage-fright problem.

3. It avoids the money and time problems of conventional theatre with its elaborate trappings and scenic effects.

4. It permits the presentation of some large-cast or difficult dramas that might not otherwise be produced because of staging difficulties.

5. It helps the participant readers develop their voices and interpretative skills, and it helps the listeners develop their imaginations.

6. It gives the church another exciting means of dramatizing the faith, teaching Christian ideals, commenting on modern society, and aiding worship. It may not replace the traditional homily but it has exciting possibilities for pushing the gospel in our world where people often turn off their heads to one-way, monological communication. As one of my correspondents wrote, "It's so much more vivid than sermons!"

Finding and Preparing Materials

The October 1971 issue of *Educational Theatre Journal* contains a list of the most-produced Readers Theatre works during the previous school year, based upon a survey of its member colleges. In order of frequency of use, the productions listed were: *Spoon River Anthology*, a haunting free-verse description of a small midwestern town by Edgar Lee Masters; *Under Milk Wood*, a humorous poetic description of a day's happenings in a Welsh village by Dylan Thomas; *John Brown's Body*, Stephen Vincent Benét's long narrative poem; *The World of Carl Sandburg*, a compilation of his writings by Norman Corwin; *Brecht on Brecht*, a compilation of the work of the East German playwright; *In White America*, a documentary play presenting American black history by Martin Duberman; *U.S.A.*, an arrangement by Paul Shyre of the famous novel by Dos Passos; and *Dandelion Wine*, adapted by Duane Hunt and Leslie Irene Coger from the novel about summer childhood by Ray Bradbury. Conspicuously absent from this year's list were the old favorites *J.B.*, Archibald MacLeish's play based on the story of Job, which many feel is just as effective as a reading, if not more so, and *A Thurber Carnival*, a compiled script representing some of the best humor of James Thurber.

This assortment of college productions shows you what kinds of material are being used for the longer shows. You may have noticed the absence of plays per se from the top eight, indicating that many find Readers Theatre more valuable for presenting other kinds of literature. Of course drama, with its inherent dialogue, conflict, and action, is most easily adapted.

Many one-act plays lend themselves to group reading and are suitable for church groups whether written by secular or avowedly Christian authors. Some of them require very little revision, such as William Saroyan's *Coming Through the Rye* or Tennessee Williams' *The Case of the Crushed Petunias* or Brochet's *The Gardener Who Was Afraid of Death*. These plays raise exciting, discussable questions about life and faith and the meaning of it all. More difficult because of their verse style are plays like Turner's *Christ in the Concrete City* or Ward's *The Holy Family* or *The Figure on the Cross*, but they can be read effectively by a skilled team —along with a host of other "religious" and "secular" dramas too numerous to mention. A selective listing of the better religious dramas may be secured from the Division of Christian Life and Mission of the National Council of Churches (see Bibliography).

Radio plays are highly adaptable, since they were written for the oral-aural dimension alone. Two examples are Stephen Vincent Benét's *A Child Is Born*, a delightfully sentimental treatment of Bethlehem from the innkeeper's point of view, and Dorothy Sayers' radio series on the life of Christ, *The Man Born to Be King*. The latter is very complex and rather difficult but sections of it could be prepared and read with great success during the church year. It is seldom done but would be well worth the effort.

Although churches are unlikely to produce a full-length play unless its content is obviously religious (such as *The Green Pastures, J.B.,* or *The Crucible),* cuttings or scenes could be taken from plays to illustrate various worship themes. The Lizzie-Starbuck dialogue in Act II of Nash's *The Rainmaker* develops the importance of believing in yourself and how this is fostered by the respect of another. The scene at Willy Loman's graveside in Arthur Miller's *Death of a Salesman* is a reflection of a man's failure to find identity and is summed up in Biff's comment about his father, "He never knew who he was." A cutting or two from Auden's Christmas oratorio, *For the Time Being,* will provide new insights during Advent. The trial in Shaw's *Saint Joan* dramatically matches a sort of Protestant individual courage against the pharisaism of the medieval religious establishment. A scene from Osborne's *Luther* or Bolt's *A Man for All Seasons* or Anouilh's *Becket* will illuminate the man of faith and conscience struggling against the political system. A piece of dialogue from Hochhuth's *The Deputy* involving the Nazi "doctor" of the extermination camp and the loving young priest who shares the fate of the persecuted Jews can illustrate human cynicism, cruelty, and altruism at the same time. Or, on Mother's Day with the theme of marriage and the home, why not use a scene from *Our Town* or selections from Mark Twain's *Adam's Diary* and *Eve's Diary?* On Children's Day pick a children's story with a message, like Jay Williams' delightful trust tale *The Cookie Tree,* and group-read it as the sermon of the day. These are just a few suggestions—the possibilities are immense. New plays and stories are constantly being written, and the person looking for Readers Theatre material to illustrate Christian themes is limited only by the size of his mind and the extent of his reading.

But drama is not the only source of material, as we've seen. Both real and fictional stories can become Readers Theatre scripts. First, consider the wide range of Biblical materials. When as a college student I heard Charles Laughton do his magnificent reading of the three men in the fiery furnace (Daniel 3), I was staggered by the power in the human voice and by the power in the story itself. It certainly helped me to appreciate the rich literature of the Old Testament, which is full of exciting dramatic narrative and vivid imagery. Group readings of the stories of Joseph, Jonah, Noah, Daniel, Job, and all the rest might really stretch people's minds. The book of Job, by the way, is drama in verse form.

In the New Testament, the Gospels contain lots of material to blow the mind and prick the heart. Again, stories involving characters and dialogue make the best Readers Theatre—an adaptation of a parable like that of the talents, a dialogue conversation such as Jesus had with Nicodemus or the woman at the well, a dramatic story of healing or the trial before Pilate or the storm at sea or the breakfast on the beach where Jesus the risen Lord appeared to his disciples. What an improvement group reading can be over the usual humdrum, monotone reading of Scripture by Parson Jones (who has slaved over his sermon for hours but hasn't rehearsed the Scripture reading once). Some editing may be necessary to make the passage more readable and to give it the flavor of an actual event. For illustration I refer you to the reading script for "The Man Born Blind" in the resource section.

Why not develop a reading script for an entire Gospel? A group reading of the story of Jesus in Matthew, say, would be exciting. Or a reading of the Passion stories culminating with the Resurrection accounts might well be the central event in Easter worship. As the readers skillfully tell the story episode by episode, the events of those days will suddenly acquire a contemporaneity and life they never had before for your congregation. Or, to suggest more creative possibilities, try using musical bridges and showing Biblical slides during the reading. You might make the bridges guitarred folk songs and use slides of our busy modern world that are relevant to the happenings described in the Gospels.

Many short stories contain spiritual insights and can be adapted for group reading to an audience. John Steinbeck's *The Pearl,* for example, would take a good deal of editing but could be well worth the trouble. *The Innovator and Other Modern Parables,* a recent collection written by G. William Jones, includes a number of thought-provoking tales, one of which is part of the resource section in this book. Humorous stories like Thurber's "A Unicorn in the Garden" and "The Secret Life of Walter Mitty" relate significant insights about human nature with the light touch. Christmas is easy—there are tons of Christmas stories that could be group-read, although very few of them are gems like Dickens' *A Christmas Carol* or O. Henry's "The Gift of the Magi" or Henry van Dyke's *The Story of the Other Wise Man.*

Cuttings from novels can often be meaningfully read. I have cut a number of exciting scenes from the Adela Rogers St. Johns novel about a modern businessman-turned-preacher, *Tell No Man,* although I've worked just one of them into worship so far. It's possible to edit an entire novel for Readers Theatre, but the process is time-consuming and very complicated because of the length of the novel and the number of characters. I doubt that a church group would be interested in adapting an entire novel unless it were a classic of Christian literature like Lloyd C. Douglas' *The Robe.* One good example of an adaptation of a novel is to be found in the Coger-White *Readers Theatre Handbook: Dandelion Wine,* by Ray Bradbury.

Poetry can be used too. Poems such as W. H. Auden's *The Age of Anxiety* and Robert Frost's "The Death of the Hired Man" have been successfully group-read. Most poetry, however, is written in a reflective, subjective vein and does not lend itself to group reading though it may be read expressively by an individual. That is, most poetry has powerful subjective meaning but lacks dramatic appeal, which is important to us. Free verse poetry like Hermann Hagedorn's *The Bomb That Fell on America,* which has characters and dialogue, makes lively group reading if skillfully prepared.

Compiled documentary Readers Theatre scripts can be fun too. Such a script may include news reports, editorials, historical documents, essays, letters, diaries, and other material. John Hersey's *Hiroshima* and Martin Duberman's *In White America* are researched documentary scripts which have significance for thoughtful Christians. A church group could develop a documentary that would describe the events surrounding the assassination of Martin Luther King, Jr., or of John F. Kennedy, for example. It would be an exciting venture to prepare a reading script about such Christian heroes as Albert Schweitzer, Clarence Jordan, or Father Damien—or perhaps William Carey or one of the other early missionaries whose lives were full of adventure. When the Christian community celebrates the life of a Christian hero in this fashion, all who listen and participate may be inspired to renew their own commitment to the Lord's ministry.

The development of such a script takes time and careful research. Although my play on Martin Niemoeller, *God Is My Fuehrer,* is a biographical drama rather than documentary as such, it contains a lot of documented material about the German pastor who organized resistance to Hitler and the Nazis. Perhaps a brief account of my research will be instructive. First I consulted Niemoeller's autobiography and the two available biographies, and made copious notes; then I looked through his published sermons and noted significantly vivid passages to include in the play. I thoroughly searched indexes to periodicals and newspapers to find articles or references to Niemoeller's activities prior to and during World War II, when he was ultimately imprisoned at Sachsenhausen and Dachau. I was particularly interested in published conversations and dialogue involving Niemoeller so that I could include many of his own words and phrases in my play.

Having done this research, I then had a body of information from which I selected an outline of events. I then developed scenes from that outline, choosing them for their dramatic qualities and potential impact on an audience as well as their biographical significance. I put these scenes together on the basis of chronological sequence, logical development, and the development of a dramatic climax, which I felt occurred when Nie-moeller personally confronted Adolf Hitler in his offices. Also, I tried to vary the number of characters from scene to scene and to vary the level of emotional intensity. An audience can't stay high indefinitely; there must be some "lows" in between, a chance to rest and reflect. Some of these low-intensity segments were chronological bridges read by the narrator; others were light or slower scenes involving characters. Ultimately I developed a biographical play that was artistically viable, I felt, and could educate and inspire an audience.

Now I've mentioned a number of things that you should consider in developing a documentary or biographical Readers Theatre script. Get to work, and let me know how you make out!

How about creating an original script? Most churches have some artistic people, possibly even professional writers, who might develop some original material for group reading. Very few manuscripts have actually been designed just for Readers Theatre. Dylan Thomas' play for voices, *Under Milk Wood*, is the only one that comes to mind. Oscar Rumpf has written some fine modern choric readings which border on Readers Theatre and illustrate how contemporary material (political slo-gans, television commercials, etc.) can be welded into an engaging, provocative script. Very timely material can be developed from reading today's newspaper—note what Arthur Hoppe and Art Buchwald do in the topical, satirical vein. Original material could be used to awaken Christian concern about such current issues as ecology, imperialism, governmental integrity, drugs, sexual behavior, and the price of bananas! The task isn't easy; perhaps it's as difficult as writing a new play, since attention must be given to characters, lively dialogue, progression of action, climax, and perhaps other elements of drama. But the results may be quite explosive.

Selecting Material: Important Questions

When you've found a piece of literature—or invented one—that you think you'd like to read, stop and ask yourself some serious questions. Number one: *Will this material accomplish our purpose on this occasion?* If the selection is to be part of worship, the question is, Will it clearly support the worship theme? Sometimes when you love a piece of litera-ture for what it means to *you*, you don't recognize that others may fail to see a clear relationship between it and the theme. Sometimes the congre-gation misses the connection if the material is too abstruse, symbolic, or satirical. In one church, for example, a dramatist put together a youth team to read the last scene from *J.B.* as part of a Christmas Eve service. She thought it had a message about incarnation, and it did—for her. Others came expecting something more traditional on Christmas Eve and failed to find the connection.

Equally important is question number two: *Will this material make good Readers Theatre?* Some literature can't be read meaningfully by a group since it lacks the qualities we've mentioned—and some literature simply defies reading aloud by anybody! If it's a dramatic piece that involves a huge cast, extensive stage business, or scenic spectacle, it would be difficult for group reading. If it's literature that's highly reflective, descriptive, or abstract, and that lacks characterization or dialogue, it's probably not for you. But if it has a message, has dialogue, logical action, and sensory appeal, if it has a limited number of well-defined characters and reads well aloud, go, man, go!

Your best material has strong evocative powers. That is, it describes very real, authentic human experience—the kinds of things you've done or know about and can identify with. (And if you can, your audience probably can.) It is absorbing material if it involves genuine persons with very real emotions engaged in human activities, enterprises, struggles, confrontations. Or, if it happens to be fantasy, it must be vivid, imaginative, and startling enough to engage your listeners. (They should not be saying, "Oh, how silly!" but "I never looked at it quite that way!")

Also, your material should have a unity, a completeness to it. There should be a significant climax, perhaps with secondary climaxes leading to it. It must leave you with a sense of finality. Not that it provides all the answers—good literature seldom does; in fact, it may well leave you wondering—but your artistic sense should be satisfied even if your intellect is gasping for breath. By analogy, a musical composition may leave you with a variety of feelings, from satisfaction to joy to despair to disgust, but it may still be *artistically* complete. But if the piece ends with a discordant note, the experience is shattering and the values in the music (unless you're one of the few people who can stand discords) are lost. A good piece of literature is not discordant in an artistic sense, although it may be very disturbing intellectually or emotionally.

So, in cutting from a long literary selection, you have to make sure your cutting is complete, that it does not leave out the important climax —which might leave the audience hanging in anticipation of a resolution that never arrives. However, most well-written scenes contain a climax that takes place near the close of the scene—often the curtain line represents the emotional summit of the scene—and if the adapter includes the closing section he will seldom go wrong.

Thirdly, you should ask, *Will this selection fit our time limit?* Your pastor may want no more than a five-minute piece read in the worship service. So you must time the piece by reading it aloud. *Aloud*—silent reading is quicker and won't give you a fair timing. (Sometimes you can read just one page aloud and calculate the time.) Most dramatic scenes can be cut, but you have to be careful what you scissor! Now, if the selection is to *be* the sermon, it probably should be about twenty minutes long—for most churches in our society. On the other hand, you may be doing an evening program of Readers Theatre. "Time's no problem," you say. Be careful! Your people will easily spend two or three hours at a sitting in a theatre, but they may not be content to sit in church much more than an hour! Why? Churchman's mentality is one answer, hard pews another. So respect the one-hour time limit unless you've got something very good and your congregation understands clearly that the program is longer. Chances are that only something famous like *Our Town* or *Cry, the Beloved Country* will hold people in church for a long evening without much restlessness.

Here's our fourth consideration: *Do we have adequate personnel for this reading?* Here's where you mentally review the people you can call on and you tick off their qualifications: "Yes, Betty, John, and Joe—they're competent, they can handle it. But what about the narrator in this one—it's tricky—and those other character parts? I'd better use the three-character scene instead." One would not give a script like *Christ in the Concrete City* to an inexperienced reading team—you'd have to have six very good interpreters. Some pieces will demand more of your readers than they can give at their stage of development. Be careful; don't tackle something too big for you. Otherwise your readers and your audience may be very disappointed.

Preparing the Script

Now and then you run across a play or a scene that doesn't require any changes to make it Readers Theatre, but most of the stuff you read will require some adaptation. Whether your material is poetry or drama, essay or story, let's consider some general rules for adapting the material.

1. **Use the author's language.** This is very important: Keep it the author's script. Don't rewrite lines or paraphrase unless you must. There are reasons for paraphrasing lines (to make a transition, to condense the narrative, to make the phrasing sound modern), but you shouldn't tackle the material with the idea of rewriting it. If it has to be totally rewritten, it's not good literature. The author, if he's good, has thoughtfully, creatively, put words together for particular auditory-cognitive-emotive effects. Respect his work—don't wreck it.

2. **Be selective.** Include only those passages which move the story forward, establish character, or describe essential action. Cut the trivial, the irrelevant, or the overly descriptive. Cutting a good piece is difficult.

Let me illustrate the cutting process. Some time ago I prepared a

Readers Theatre script of C. S. Lewis' *The Great Divorce* for a college chapel program. (A piece of my adaptation appears in the resource section.) At first glance nothing in the story seemed dull or irrelevant, so how could I edit it? Still, I knew that something had to give if it was to be condensed into a fifty-minute program. On re-reading, I found that some of the material was less vivid or less important to the story than other sections, so I edited out some passages on that basis. Also, I dropped a few scenes (conversations between Spirits and Ghosts) which were not as moving as others, and I pared down the narrative parts so that only the thread of narrative telling the story and introducing the scenes was retained— none of Lewis' diversions or digressions, by and large, were included. In the opening section—a description of an "excursion" by bus from the nebulous "Grey Town"—I deleted some passages which the story line didn't require, plus anything that restated an old idea (one already mentioned in the story).

In adapting dialogue from such a story, phrases like "he said" can be dropped out. Adverbial phrases treating an attitude or tone of voice can be deleted, since that will be clear from the way it's read:

> "What isn't true?" ~~asked the Ghost sulkily~~.
>
> "You!" ~~gasped the Ghost~~. "*You* have the face to tell *me* I wasn't a decent chap?"[1]

Words like "sulkily" or "gasping" can be added to the script parenthetically to instruct the reader as to vocal tone, etc. There are very few cases where the "he said" or "she exclaimed" might be retained. One case might be the narrative speech that opens the reading and introduces the characters:

> **NARRATOR.** In Osborne's controversial play *Luther*, the young reformer is being interviewed in Augsburg by the papal legate, Cardinal Cajetan, prior to Luther's formal examination at Worms. We pick up the scene as Martin cries out . . . (*leading in to Luther's opening speech in that scene*).

Or, the "he saids" of a story may be retained if they enhance the comic effect:

> **SHE.** "Herman,"
> **NARRATOR.** She said, in tones of sugarplum sweetness.
> **HE.** "Yes, dear,"
> **NARRATOR.** He replied, with weary resignation.
> **SHE.** "I wish I could be happy."
> **NARRATOR.** He looked up from his paper briefly before pulling it down about his ears.

HE. "So do I, dear,"
NARRATOR. He mumbled.

When the narrative lines reinforce the character's attitude or vocal tone, the effect is often humorous. In *Old Ymir's Clay Pot* by Norman Dietz, the "ands," "saids," and parenthetical remarks interposed between dialogue lines strengthen the fanciful, haunting imagery of this delightful fable:

OLD MAN. It was finished, and Old Ymir sighed and smiled and went to bed.

MAN. He slept fitfully that night, tossing and turning in the darkness, and awoke next morning without rest, to fret and pace in large impatient circles through the days that followed while the new clay cured and dried. And then when the intolerable wait was over, with the first faint light of morning on that day of days, he hurried over to the kiln and took out the bowl. Proudly he placed it on the counter, and all over the shop all the other pots and bowls and plates and crocks and cups said

GIRL. "Oh!"

MAN. And

GIRL. "Ah!"

MAN. And

GIRL. "My how beautiful!"

MAN. For it was a masterpiece. Then no one said anything. But Old Ymir was smiling.

GIRL. "Hello!"

MAN. Said the little pot finally.

GIRL. For in those days pots could talk like people.[2]

The Dietz piece, of course, was written for voices, but I am suggesting that you might follow much the same pattern in adapting Thurber or other light or satirical material.

In adapting *The Great Divorce* I not only omitted certain scenes but cut a few pieces of dialogue from scenes we used. This dialogue, while interesting, was expendable. The result was a shorter, tighter story which moved more quickly than the original, holding the audience's interest from start to finish. (Most of the audience, anyway.)

To examine the selection process from the perspective of documentary material, let's see how one adapter prepared John Hersey's *Hiroshima* for Readers Theatre.

As no one else has succeeded in doing, Mr. Hersey makes real what the first atomic bomb used on human beings was like—what atomic power can mean in terms of destruction of human lives and plans. He does this by making it possible for the imagination to begin to grasp what happened in Hiroshima. He was able to illustrate the general facts wih the experiences of six human beings—what they were doing that morning, what they thought at the moment of the explosion, what they say, and what had happened to them a year later. Each report represents the experiences of a person who is somewhat typical of a group that might be found in any modern city—the poor widowed mother, the man of religion, the scientifically trained doctor, and so on. Also they represent reactions of survivors at increasing distances from the center of the explosion. This skillful combination of individual reactions, together with general over-all facts, is the technique by which we are enabled to visualize events clearly.

Because of the article's special importance at this time, also because of the excellence of its composition, it was selected for reading at one of the regular Wednesday afternoon interpretative reading presentations at the University of California. As a result of its effectiveness at that presentation various organizations in the San Francisco Bay Area requested additional readings. The requests continued throughout the school year; we averaged almost a reading a week. The following is a report of the development of this project.

Plan of the Reading. The first chapter introduces six people who were survivors of the bomb. A narrator read the introductory and transitional materials. Then as each of the individual stories was presented a different reader took up the reporting. This helped keep the reports distinct and also gave variety to the reading.

Arranging and Cutting. The report is a shocking, intense experience. When read silently it is possible to sustain intensity for a longer period of time than when listening. To project the purpose of the report and maintain the dramatic unity, about 50 minutes of material was selected. After trial this was reduced even further to about 37 minutes plus a four-minute introduction.

The reports of one person, Dr. Fujii, were omitted as not being essential to the idea since the reports of Dr. Sasaki of the large, modern Red Cross hospital served to represent more emphatically the dissolution of scientific planning and medical care.

Several of the more gruesome parts were omitted on the theory that they became anticlimactic and hence destructive of the impact desired. When listening one cannot respond repeatedly to stimuli of equal intensity.

Miss Toshiko Sasaki was called Miss Toshiko to avoid confusion with Dr. Sasaki; there was no significance in their having the same surnames.

The only rearrangement of material thought necessary was that the first report of each survivor was given in a sequence according to his distance from the center of the explosion. This was done for simplicity and clarity.[3]

3. Employ narration skillfully. Usually Readers Theatre requires some sort of narration. Even a drama read without changes may require some introduction, and most plays have stage directions or physical business which may have to be narrated when the play is read. You should avoid using a narrator extensively, however, since dialogue between characters is more interesting. Sometimes you can add a word or phrase or sentence to the dialogue that clarifies the action taking place. At other times the action or business may be complicated, and so you will have the narrator explain what is taking place. Let me illustrate this with a scene from Victor Hugo's novel *Les Misérables* which is printed in the resource section, namely, the famous incident of Jean Valjean and the Bishop's candle-sticks. The convict has boldly entered the Bishop's house looking for food and lodging for the night. After he identifies himself, showing the Bishop his "passport" which indicates his convict status, Jean Valjean realizes that he is addressing a priest. Then the narrative says: "While speaking, he had deposited his knapsack and stick in the corner, replaced his passport in his pocket, and sat down." Since that is important information, I decided to keep it; since the line describes several actions, I decided to have the narrator deliver it verbatim. If the statement had instead read, "Having said this, Jean Valjean wearily sat down," it would been better included in the dialogue. I could have tacked it onto the beginning of Jean's next speech:

> **JEAN.** *May I please sit down? (With an exhausted sigh.)* You are humane, Monsieur Curé; you don't despise me. A good priest is a good thing. Then you don't want me to pay you?

Actually, with the narrative line removed—if there were no other action to describe at that point—the interpolation would come in the middle of a longer speech by Jean and the suggested act of sitting down would break up that speech nicely.

Many presentations will demand lots of narration—especially those adapted from stories or novels. In my adaptation of *The Great Divorce* I kept the narration in the first person, since the author intended it to sound as if he himself were recounting his adventures. I set aside one reader as the narrator (who also read the dialogue lines in which the storyteller himself was involved). In most stories the narration is written in the third person, generally in the past tense but occasionally in the present tense. Since the present tense suggests immediacy, currency, and spontaneity, it often works well in Readers Theatre. But if the author has written the account in the past tense, it's unlikely you'll want to change it.

Narration has many uses in Readers Theatre. It is useful in present-ing important descriptive material, for setting the scene or making transi-tions from one scene to another, for introducing characters and describing action, and even to interpret and reflect on action being taken. In adapt-ing a story you have basically three options in terms of the narrative material. If the story is primarily written in dialogue, you might decide to revise and add to the characters' lines whatever explanatory comment is necessary to clarify the action. But it's unlikely that you'll be able to reduce everything to dialogue satisfactorily, and if you did, the result could be ludicrous. The second and third options are more viable.

The second method is the simplest and often the best: Ascribe the narrative lines to the character who is speaking, has just spoken, or is presently the prime mover, but without making them part of the spoken dialogue. To illustrate with a passage from O. Henry's "The Gift of the Magi":

JIM. Jim looked around the room curiously. "You say your hair is gone?" he said, with an air almost of idiocy.

DELLA. "You needn't look for it," said Della. "It's sold, I tell you—sold and gone, too. It's Christmas Eve, boy. Be good to me, for it went for you. Maybe the hairs of my head were numbered," she went on with a sudden serious sweetness, "but nobody could ever count my love for you. Shall I put the chops on, Jim?"

JIM. Out of his trance Jim seemed quickly to wake. He enfolded his Della.

Even here one might delete adverbial phrases, etc., retaining only the essential narration. "She went on with a sudden serious sweetness" would be embodied in the reader's voice, so it could be omitted, whereas "Out of his trance . . ." describes important action and would be retained.

The other method of using narration is to assign all of the non-dialogue material to a separate reader, probably paring down to the essential action:

NARRATOR. Jim looked around the room curiously.

JIM. You say your hair is gone?

DELLA. You needn't look for it. It's sold, I tell you—sold and gone, too. It's Christmas Eve, boy. Be good to me, for it went for you. Maybe the hairs of my head were numbered, but nobody could ever count my love for you. Shall I put the chops on, Jim?

NARRATOR. Out of his trance Jim seemed quickly to wake. He enfolded his Della.

In some pieces there is so much description that it justifies using more than one narrator. Dylan Thomas' *Under Milk Wood* is written for two. The Readers Theatre adaptation by Nelson Bond of Orwell's *Animal Farm* has all seven readers serving as narrators at times, while assuming roles at other times. Often it's artistic to make it appear as if the entire cast is telling the tale. And if you're adapting poetic material or a work that is strongly sensory or reflective, you may want to assign narrative material to a number of voices. This gives a variety of vocal effects and makes for an interesting flow:

MAN 1.   And everyone lived in the style of life to which he aspired—

MAN 2.   Except for the poor people—

MAN 3.   And it was easy to keep them out of sight.

WOMAN. Out of sight, out of mind. Right?

MEN. *(With assurance.)* Right!

WOMAN. Anyway, if they're poor, it just has to be their own fault. Right?

MEN. *(Swinging their fists.)* Right!

ALL. *(After a pause.)* And the end of life was possessions, and the god of life was the Great God Thing.[4]

4. Identify characters carefully. This means a number of things. One is simply that your script should make it clear to the audience who is in the scene and who is speaking. Often characters will be introduced by narration—even so, it is helpful to have them call each other by name (write it into the dialogue) as they begin talking, and to use each other's names several times during the scene. Make it easy for your audience!

There are some other character concerns. In adapting a play or story you will need as many characters as are essential. If one of them is not essential to your scene or passage, or has only a line or two, perhaps it should be omitted or written into the narrative instead of being assigned a reader. It's distracting to have people on stage who are largely silent, and it's perplexing to an audience to hear a line or two that's not essential and is hard to connect with a character. Also, you may want to arrange the material so that the readers have nearly an equivalent number of speeches. Sometimes you can give the one line a character may have to someone else who figures prominently in the scene. In doing a particular scene from *Luther*, the reading team found that Tetzel appeared at the very end of the scene and said only "Yes?" so his part was written into the part of Cardinal Cajetan who said, looking off, "Ah, Tetzel . . . What? . . . No, he didn't recant" (as if answering Tetzel's unheard question). There was no point in making a reader Tetzel just to read that scene!

You may want to give a reader more than one character's lines to read when (a) there are many characters, (b) there are more characters than available voices, (c) you want to keep the staging as simple as possible or you are reading in a very cramped area, or (d) you want to use only your most capable readers. In a very long or a large-cast story you may find your readers assuming several roles each. Characters may be given to readers according to the importance of the character and the skill of the readers, according to the character's place in the story, his relationship to the other characters, or various other factors, including appearance, age, and gender.

In adapting *The Great Divorce*, I had just seven readers to work with—and I preferred to work with those seven rather than enlarge the cast, anyway, for artistic reasons. Fortunately, the minimum number required by the text seemed to be seven: five men and two women. Each voice had to interpret several characters. I tried to spread the load so that each reader would have a relatively equal number of roles and scenes to portray, but the women did come out second best. I tried also to avoid having a reader appear in two successive scenes, and I kept the Spirit and Ghost parts separate throughout—although a reader might read two or three different Ghosts, he would not read a Spirit. (All this to help the audience keep the character clearly in mind.) Everyone, of course, was involved in the opening scene, which was the bus trip from "Grey Town," since that gave it the feeling of a busful of passengers. Also, to give more strength to the female side, I revised one of the scenes so that a Ghost "brother" became instead the sister of one of the Spirits; without changing much dialogue, this gave us one all-woman scene and added variety to the production.

Assigning characters to readers is a complicated business when you're adapting a script. You want to be creative and economical in doing so, but you must make sure that the characters can be clearly known to the audience even when readers are slipping in and out of several different roles.

5. Use special sound effects when desirable. Certain selections might benefit from using a metronome to indicate the inexorable passage of time, a gong to suggest an Oriental setting, marching feet to indicate preparation for battle, a whistle to identify the entrance of the police— or whatever. In reading the very last episode in *A Man for All Seasons,* we added a drumbeat under part of the dialogue to build to the climax of Sir Thomas More's martyrdom on the scaffold. In Bond's adaptation of *Animal Farm* he suggests using music from Saint-Saëns's *Carnival of the Animals* to make transitions and suggest mood. Creative adapters will find many ways to use auditory devices like these to enhance the message. They must, of course, be appropriate and not overdone; otherwise they will distract the audience and detract from the meanings in the literature.

Also, the interpreters' voices can be used in unusual ways. Here's a description of the creative vocal effects used in the Hunt-Coger adaptation of Bradbury's novel *Dandelion Wine:*

> Many vocalized sound devices were used in this production of *Dandelion Wine.* When Doug lay ill and the day seemed interminable, one

voice ticked off the time while other voices told of the scenes going through Doug's fevered brain. The sound of this relentless ticking counterpointed the rising excitement in the other voices as the fever caused wilder and wilder ideas to surge through Doug's mind. The scene was climaxed by voices singing "Shall We Gather at the River?" in harmony at first, then in the discordant sounds that the feverish Doug was presumably hearing. Singing was also introduced when Colonel Freeleigh was recalling Civil War songs. As each song came to Colonel Freeleigh's mind, a voice sang a portion of it, as though far away.[5]

6. Make the reading script usable. The script should be easy to read and easy to handle. It should be carefully typed or printed in large letters, with good margins and plenty of space for making notes during rehearsals. It could be double-spaced; lacking that, provide an extra space between speeches. Note the identity of the readers for the speeches in capital letters on the lefthand side (NARRATOR, VOICE 6, MARTIN, SERVANT, etc.). It's probably better to use bond paper; inferior paper or onionskin tends to rustle when turned, and if the paper is quite thin the printing on the next sheet may show through.

The reading scripts will not be seen by the audience if lecterns are used; otherwise they will be held in plain sight by the readers. To give the group a uniform look and make a pleasing appearance, put the readers' scripts in identical folders. Probably they should be the same color, although in some cases you may wish to indicate something symbolic by giving certain readers folders of a variant color.

You will be pressed for time, of course—everyone is—but don't do a careless job of preparing the reading scripts. The script is an important tool. If it's poorly prepared, either in content or in readability, the team effort may suffer, the oral effect may be hampered, and the spiritual impact diminished.

Once you have a powerful, readable script—and enough copies for every cast member plus director and assistants—you're ready to begin casting and rehearsals. So now we turn to some of the factors involved in effective oral interpretation.

Developing Capable Interpreters

If the group has a good script and a date to perform, then whoever's directing needs to cast and rehearse his reading team. It would be nice if he could just advertise a time for auditioning in the church bulletin, then sit back and wait for the crowd to break down his door. If only he could choose readers from thirty people instead of the three who may show up! Realistically, in church life you have to go out and buttonhole and convince your "volunteers" that you have a beautiful thing going and that they can find the time for just one more church project!

Some people steer clear of anything called "theatre" but if they're approached on the basis of "reading a part," which doesn't sound quite as frightening, they may consider it. But, please—don't approach people with the line, "It's *just* a reading." To be fair, tell them at the outset that your project will involve hours of rehearsal and that the director will settle for nothing less than everyone's best effort. We are assuming that your performance has a purpose beyond entertainment, so you can approach people in terms of it's being another type of ministry in the service of God.

Unfortunately, good readers are hard to find these days—especially male ones! Good readers, remember, are not born; they are trained. Hopefully, people have been trained in grade school to read aloud well; unfortunately, with many it doesn't seem to "take" or the training is deficient. But you can help people develop these skills using some of the ideas in this chapter.

In some ways, and for many people, reading aloud is more difficult than acting. Some people can look and sound rather natural once they've memorized their lines, but put a book in front of them and they sound like they're reading—which is exactly what we don't want! So don't be completely discouraged if you're the director and most of your volunteers read very woodenly at first. Work with them. Who knows, from your group another Charles Laughton may emerge!

Normally, church groups will select small-cast scripts; even so, you may have trouble filling the cast if Readers Theatre is new to your church. On the other hand, you may have more aspirants than you have parts; if that happens, Readers Theatre has arrived! You can be a bit more selective. At any rate, you will cast your script with these considerations in view: (1) how fluently the individual reads and how flexible his voice seems to be, (2) how industrious and dependable he is, (3) whether his personal schedule seems to be harmonious with projected rehearsals, (4) establishing a vocal variety in your cast so that all your readers don't sound alike, and (5) correlating the reader's personality with the role he is to interpret. This last point is not as important as the others, since in many performances the individual interprets more than one role anyway. A good reader is flexible enough to interpret a wide variety of characters.

If you have to exclude some volunteers from your cast this time, try to involve them next time around. Of course, you won't want to load your cast with too many inexperienced people; a healthy mixture of veterans and tyros is welcome.

Rehearsals

No one in the cast should get a special dispensation; everyone should commit himself to the rehearsal schedule, which may be finalized with the approval of the cast. The amount of rehearsal time will vary according to the difficulty of the script and its length, plus the experience and skill of the readers. Readers who are veteran performers will need much less rehearsal time than a cast containing several beginners. Using capable, experienced interpreters, I have found that a medium-difficulty dramatic scene of ten minutes requires about an hour and a half of rehearsal time for best results. (You can whip it up in less time but it won't come out as well!) When I speak of rehearsal time I'm including both actual reading rehearsal and discussing the problems which the group is encountering in its reading. Two or three good readers may be able to prepare something in shorter time, but you'd better plan on at least nine minutes of rehearsal time per minute of performance time. If the cast is weak or inexperienced, or if the script is very complicated or requires unusual sound devices or other effects, rehearsal time may be doubled. In rehearsing short readings for worship, our church group has usually spent the previous Sunday's church-school hour in rehearsal—and sometimes we've had to start two weeks early to develop a five- or ten-minute reading! It's always good to plan one more rehearsal than you think you'll need. Emergencies may blossom or illness may force cancellation of a rehearsal. It's wiser to plan too much rehearsal time than too little, obviously. On the other hand, don't overdo it to the point where the cast loses interest and gets stale by the time the performance comes along.

If possible, readers should have the script well in advance of the first rehearsal, with instructions to read it through and try to understand it as a total piece. The reader should be told what part he is to prepare, and maybe he should come to the first rehearsal with a detailed character description in mind. Then at the outset the readers could comment on their understanding of character, mood, message, and meaning. Discussing these issues together would provide a basis for team effort and good interpretation as the rehearsals get under way.

If we're talking about a big production requiring several rehearsals, the first or second would tend to be exploratory. The director should give some basic guidance concerning focus, positioning, stress, timing, and other matters, or the group may work out those problems together if they have time. Often the director will stop the reading to ask someone, "How do you see that line?" or "What is your emotional involvement at this point, Betty?" or "Why did you emphasize *taught* in that sentence, Joe?" The director may make all decisions about interpretation himself, but it's better to work them out with the readers if they're crucial. The director should try to stimulate the evaluative mechanism in his readers' minds and bring them to a thoughtful consideration of why and how their lines should be read.

Later rehearsals are for polishing the performance. By then readers understand their lines, and they're beginning to express themselves gracefully. The director will be helping them with physical expression, trying to keep them alive and responding facially and kinetically to the action even when they are not speaking.

By the last two rehearsals the director will be talking about time and climax, and making sure that there is a unity and completeness to each scene and to the work as a whole. In addition, he will be listening from various points in the auditorium to make sure that everyone is audible. At least one rehearsal should be held in the place of performance. At that time the staging should be exactly as it is planned for performance, and any costuming or lighting touches should be tried out so the director may judge their effect.

The Interpreter as a Bridge

I've been trying to give you some idea of the director's task in a Readers Theatre effort. Now let's think about the individual reader.

The reader-interpreter is someone who has found a particular literary piece so meaningful that, like an evangelist, he wants to share it with others. As he does, the author's work is now expanded and made tangible for an audience. The author may not be present, and could not present the material as well as the reading team even if he were present, so the reader becomes a bridge between author and audience. And since the reader is translating the written word into audible and visual signals, he really becomes a co-creator with the author.

If he wants to pay his debt to the author, and interpret the piece meaningfully, the reader tries to discover what the author intended in writing it, what he meant to describe, symbolize, or state—what message he was sending, if any. This may require some research; the interpreter will seek to discover what kinds of assumptions and experiences led the author to write as he did. The reader's search may eventually lead him to change his mind about how to interpret the piece.

Paul Hunsinger gives a vivid illustration of this point in his book on oral interpretation.[1] A casual, unresearched knowledge of the poem "Invictus" by William Henley might give an interpreter the wrong steer, for the lines suggest the idea that Henley was a strong, bold man standing astride the cosmos:

> Out of the night that covers me,
>   Black as the Pit from pole to pole,
> I thank whatever gods may be
>   For my unconquerable soul.
>
>   . . . . .
>
> It matters not how strait the gate,
>   How charged with punishments the scroll,
> I am the master of my fate;
>   I am the captain of my soul.

But research reveals that Henley was not physically strong. On the contrary, he was a sickly child from birth, suffering from a disease of the bone which led to the amputation of one leg and threatened the other. Apparently Henley spent much of his life seriously crippled and hospitalized. This poem was written during a hospital stay between August 1873 and April 1875. With these facts, we may infer something quite different about the author's intention. Perhaps he was trying to give himself courage in this poem, struggling toward a sense of worth and fulfillment, and hopeful of eventual release from his prison of pain. So we see that background information helps us understand the author and interpret the selection according to his intentions.

The reader will study the passage and determine the intent of the author, if possible. Many times, of course, it's not possible to determine just what the author meant, so the reader interprets it in a way that makes sense to him. At other times the author's purpose is crystal clear. For example, someone reading from the Gospel of Luke would be guided by the statement of purpose which begins the account:

> Inasmuch as many have undertaken to compile a narrative of the things which have been accomplished among us, just as they were delivered to us by those who from the beginning were eyewitnesses and ministers of the word, it seemed good to me also, having followed all things closely for some time past, to write an orderly account for you, most excellent Theophilus, that you may know the truth concerning the things of which you have been informed.[2]

The reading team might seek additional information about Luke—who he was and what his relation to the Christian movement was—and then examine particular passages to discover his assumptions and biases. In reading his account of the miracles, for example, you would need to decide whether Luke personally believed in demons, whether he as a physician accepted the notion of psychosomatic illness, or whether he felt that Jesus' cures were mainly psychological rather than physical. This would affect the way you interpret the gospel accounts.

Most writers don't spell out their intentions as did Luke. If you press an author to reveal the "message" in his art he may say, "If I could spell it out in so many words there would have been no point in writing this poem" (or play, novel, essay, short story). But while an author may not set out with a message in mind, he will generally end up with one. Some attitude, assumption, claim, some approach to life, some thematic ideas are likely to rise to the surface out of all that experience which the writer brings to his task. So the interpreter scrutinizes the literature to determine what the message is.

Studying the Literature: Theme, Mood, Imagery, Climax

The reader should develop some impression of the *theme* of the passage. The theme is the important meaning which can be expressed in a single phrase or sentence. It may be "Love has the power to transform even the most hardened life," as in the episode of the bishop's candlesticks of *Les Misérables*, or "It is better to die for Christ than to live a lie," which is what I make out of the Brochet play *The Gardener Who Was Afraid of Death*. The theme of Lewis' fantasy *The Great Divorce* is a bit harder to encapsulate but it may be: "There is a huge chasm between heaven and hell, and we are constantly making choices that affect our eternal destiny." These are possible themes; there may be many subthemes or incidental motifs but all are subordinate to the overriding concern or theme. If it is expressed textually through the dialogue it won't be hard to catch, but often writers express themselves obliquely, in which case the theme may be subtextual rather than textual. But it has to be found—if you're not sure what the message is, why present it? If the reading is ambiguous to you it may well baffle your audience, too.

The theme can be distinguished from the *plot* and the central *action* of a dramatic piece. The plot is the network of happenings or episodes which provide the outline of the story. The action of the story is the central movement of the play, usually seen through the protagonist, the central figure. For example, the central action of Oedipus is that he seeks the truth and his search ultimately drives him to a discovery of his own guilt; perhaps the theme is "man cannot escape the inexorable fate set for him." The action is stated in terms of events and the purpose of the protagonist—his compelling motivation—while the theme is put in terms of the meaning or conclusion to be drawn from it all. The central action is generally obvious but the theme is often subtly concealed. But the reading team should arrive at a consensus of what the theme might be, or members may be interpreting the piece at cross-purposes.

Mood is the emotional coloring of the literature. There will be an overall emotional tone, be it joy, hatred, revenge, depression, elation, or sorrow. There will also be submoods associated with particular scenes or passages. The readers need to discuss these moods and the part they have to play in establishing them. Perhaps the important question is, What feeling do we leave with the audience at the close? Sometimes the closing mood is mixed, such as the joy-in-sorrow associated with the death of a Christian hero like Joan of Arc, Sir Thomas More, Billy Budd, or the first-century Christian in *The Gardener Who Was Afraid of Death*. The interpreter in such cases would be wary of acquiring a dolorous tone even though someone is being killed.

Imagery refers to language which appeals to the senses. Phrases like "delightful bacony smells wafted upstairs," "the foaming blues and greens of the restless sea collided with our frail craft," and "some fell among thorns, and the thorns grew with it and choked it" speak to or through the senses—sight, hearing, smell, touch, taste. The images are real to us insofar as they evoke experiences or parts of experiences we've had. So the effective reader may be one whose experiences enable him to sympathize, understand, and identify with the person or event being described. Theoretically, a Midwesterner who had never been near a ship would have difficulty interpreting *The Old Man and the Sea*, or any marine tale. However, if he reads widely and watches movies and television, the interpreter through this secondhand experience may be able to evoke images that help him to visualize Hemingway's story. The interpreter, whatever the story, will let the lines trigger his memory and recall experiences that make him relate better to his script. The director can assist him in this.

To illustrate: A college student in one of my oral interpretation classes wrote an analysis of the imagery in Edgar Allan Poe's "The Masque of the Red Death," which she was to read to the class. Notice how she recalled specific personal events that helped her relate to events or images in the story:

> "sharp pains and sudden dizziness": reminds me of one who suddenly collapses, a heart attack . . .
>
> "strong and lofty walk": reminds me of the impressiveness of Fort Ticonderoga as a child . . .
>
> "stained glass": impressions of beautiful church windows . . .
>
> "brazier of fire": reminds me of a hamburger stand at which I ate this summer . . .
>
> "gaudy and fantastic appearance": reminds me of the fears I had as a child when left alone in the kitchen where the light reflections from cars danced around the walls where the cars passed by . . .

"gigantic clock of ebony": reminds me of the huge clock which used
    to stand in my grandmother's living room . . .

"the dagger dropped": reminds me of the time one of the neighbor-
    hood boys approached my father with a drawn gun but dropped
    it when my father started to move toward him . . .

Such reflective thinking gives the interpreter insight into the images within the literature. If the readers in this way begin to visualize the
scene and experience it with their senses, the audience will almost certainly do so. This is what Lowrey and Johnson call "thinking with one's
senses,"[4] and it's very important if the performance is to acquire an au-
thenticity.

Climax is related to rhythm and timing. Every piece has a particular rhythm; there is a rise and fall of emotional intensity which may be
regular or irregular. The points of high emotional intensity are the climaxes, and there may be several minor climaxes as well as a major climax
within a work of twenty to thirty minutes' length. In a long dramatic piece,
each scene will have its own climax, although one particular scene may
promise and provide the major climax.

Another way of looking at climax is to say that when there is a major
turning point in the action, or when a certain outcome becomes inevitable, a climax is reached. This is sometimes termed the *logical* climax as
opposed to the *emotional* climax. In many dramatic selections these will
coincide. In most poetry there is no logical climax similar to the turning
point in a play—but the emotional climax is there. Whatever the literature, the reading team must develop a feel for where the climaxes occur;
often a consensual feeling about this develops from reading it together,
without anything being said. The pace usually accelerates toward a climax,
then slows down after the climax is past before beginning to build toward
the next one. This is the rhythmical pattern of literature—and life.

The Interpreter's Vocal Tools

The four basic factors of the human voice are quality, loudness, rate,
and pitch. *Quality* is that vocal sound which is peculiar to an individual;
we use labels like hoarse, thin, whining, nasal, husky, or resonant to describe a particular voice quality. Physiologically, quality is a function of the
structure of the vocal mechanism, mainly the size and shape of the person's larynx and his resonating cavities. Although one's distinct vocal quality remains constant to the extent that voiceprints are being used as well
as fingerprints to identify people, some persons can disguise their voices
well enough to imitate the qualities of others. The interpreter may want
to employ different voice qualities to suggest characters. A thin voice may
suggest weakness, idiocy, fatigue, or the voice of a child; a guttural voice

may suggest coarseness or anger or a foreign accent; a whining or nasal voice may suggest irritation or complaint; a full resonant voice will suggest confidence or authority.

Loudness is the intensity of the voice measured in decibels. We speak of raising or lowering the volume. The reader will find that a number of factors may force him to increase loudness, aside from his interpretation of the lines—such things as the number of auditors, the size of the room, the age of his audience (are there people wearing hearing aids?), and the amount of extraneous noise. The latter seems very obvious but I'm amazed at the number of readers who don't bother to raise their voices when the rain is beating on the roof or the heavy trucks are rumbling by the open windows! Of course, the interpreter employs loudness to suggest his characters' feelings as he reads. Keep in mind that contrast is the key. An interpreter who constantly reads in a loud voice may have no way to emphasize his anger later in the performance; moving suddenly from a moderate tone to a loud voice or from a loud voice to a whisper will capture attention because of the change and contrast.

Rate is speech speed and it can be measured in words per minute. Most people read at a slower rate than they converse, which is fortunate. Research indicates that people are speaking and reading faster than they did twenty years ago. This is probably not very surprising when you think about the high-speed, high-tension world in which we now live. Be wary of speaking so fast that you're unintelligible. Also, as an interpreter you will employ different rates to suggest character and give emotional coloring to your lines. Certain moods like gaity, elation, and anticipation will call for relatively fast speech rates, while such moods as loneliness, despair, and exhaustion may require slower speeds. Unfortunately, when some readers are asked to slow down, they respond by adding additional pauses to their lines; this results in a staccato speech pattern. When you slow your rate of speech, increase the duration of your sounds (riiiight!) as well as the pauses between words or phrases.

Pitch is the placement of a tone on the musical scale. People speak at different pitch levels. Also, individuals vary in the extent of their pitch range. The monotone voice, because of its very narrow pitch range, makes a very dull reader. The interpreter may work at extending his range by devising exercises for himself like the following: (a) Hum two distinct tones, then extend them farther and farther up and down the scale in opposite directions, as far as you can go. (b) Count from the lowest pitch you can muster for "One!" up the scale as high as you can go. Try this daily and see if you can make it into a higher range. Of course, singing helps. It is possible to achieve a speaking range of an octave and a half but most Americans never begin to work it. The British do better!

In spoken English we normally use three pitch levels, plus a fourth for special emphasis, on occasion:

4 extra emphasis
3 emphasis
2 normal or starting pitch
1 terminals (end of phrase)

We usually end our declarative sentences with a falling pitch, or falling terminal. We usually end our questions with a rising terminal. Sentences may be diagramed to indicate the pitch patterns.

		3		3			3				3	
2	2	Abel	2	brother?		2	Lord 2	2	2	holy	2	
Where	is		your			The		is	in	his	tem	1
												ple.

You might learn two other terms connected with pitch: inflection and intonation. *Inflection* is used to describe a pitch change or glide within a particular sound, while *intonation* refers to the pitch pattern of a sentence or longer unit of utterance. For example, we speak of a singsong intonation, meaning that the pitch pattern employed by the reader is too regular to be interesting—it puts you to sleep. Guard against developing a very regular or repetitious intonational pattern in your reading.

Inflection is extremely important in spoken English. We get meaning from each others' inflections as well as from the words themselves. *No*, for example, can be said in different inflections to express different shades of meaning. A falling inflection (N͡o) indicates certainty unless duration is prolonged, a rising inflection (N͜o) implies surprise or asks a question, an even inflection (N͞o) may suggest exasperation, and a circumflex inflection (N͡o or N͜o), where the pitch rises and falls again, or vice versa, will suggest various other meanings in context. Experiment with the exclamation "Oh!" using different inflections. Imagine that a friend has just said to you, "My husband lost his job today." Say "Oh!" to mean:

1. Pity. ("But he was getting along so well and he's such a wonderful guy.")
2. Inattention. ("I didn't quite hear you because I have some other things on my mind. What?")
3. Disbelief. ("That can't be true! I understood they weren't going to lay off anybody.")
4. Shock and fear. ("That's terrible. Maybe *my* husband'll be next!")
5. Wariness. ("Oh, no, she's going to ask me for another loan.")
6. Disgust. ("Well, I figured that bum would lose his job eventually.")
7. Delight. ("As a matter of fact, he had it coming to him. Serves him right!")

Phrasing and Stress

Phrasing is the use of pauses to set off units of discourse. A phrase is a group of related words, a thought unit. A pause is a period of silence that follows a phrase or sentence. The pause serves at least four purposes: (1) It gives the reader a chance to breathe; (2) it gives him time to look ahead in his script for the next phrase or sentence; (3) it gives the listener a brief moment to absorb what's been said; (4) it provides a clue to meaning.

As a matter of fact, an audience may or may not understand a particular line because of the phrasing. How often have you heard worship leaders read this sentence from Luke with but a brief pause after "haste," and no other pausing:

> And they went with haste / and found Mary and Joseph and the babe lying in a manger.[5]

Reading it that way puts all three of them in the manger! Obviously the sentence requires more verbal punctuation to bring out the proper meaning: a pause after Joseph to show that only the babe is in the manger! (Actually the text has a comma after Joseph, which implies that a pause is required.)

Stress is vocal emphasis. Usually we emphasize at least one key word in each phrase. Stress is a function of loudness, pitch, pause, and gesture. Say aloud with feeling, "What's the big *idea*?" putting stress on the last word. You've probably increased the loudness of that word, said it with a higher pitch, hesitated slightly before saying it, and gestured with your hands as well. All of this underlines the importance of that word and brings out the meaning you intend to convey. Emphasis in the following sentence has been indicated by underlining those words which seem to carry the meaning:

> And they <u>went</u> with <u>haste</u> // and found <u>Mary</u> and <u>Joseph</u> / and the <u>babe</u> lying in a <u>manger</u>.

Although in a word of more than one syllable (e.g., *manger*) we accent a particular syllable rather than the entire word, for our purposes we'll just say that we stress the word. The pattern of emphasis we use, which we do naturally in conversation, is a way by which we point the meaning of a particular utterance. Certain words are idea carriers; they bear the semantic baggage and must be stressed to convey meaning. Take Jesus' cryptic injunction to Peter in John 21:17; by stressing different words you can develop three possible shades of meaning:

> "*Feed* my sheep." ("Give them something really nourishing, like the gospel. Man does not live by bread alone!")

> "Feed *my* sheep." ("These followers are of particular concern to me.

Take care of them because you love *me!*")

"Feed my *sheep.*" ("Not the goats—the sheep! Don't worry about those who will not accept salvation.")

"Speak conversationally" may be the best advice to give on emphasis, since oral reading is essentially an enlarged conversation. In conversation—and in oral interpretation—we seem to follow these general rules of stress:

1. Emphasize the idea carriers, not the unimportant words. Usually they're nouns, but not always. Sometimes the verbs should be stressed because they describe the action. Sometimes adjectives should be stressed because of a distinction or comparison being made by the author, or because of their descriptive power. Adverbs or pronouns may be stressed on occasion. You would almost never stress a conjunction like "and" or the article "the," although in speaking of the Bible we may refer to it as *The* Book, in which case we stress the article to imply that the following noun is supreme (the most important book in the world). But it's disheartening to hear adults repeatedly stressing articles such as "a" or "an" in their reading. This is a carry-over from childhood reading exercises ("John has *a* dog"). Such words as "a," "an," and "the" should be unstressed so that salient words will stand out. In "The Lord is my shepherd," you might stress either "my" or "shepherd" along with "Lord," and conceivably you could emphasize "is" to strengthen the sense of currency and power in the relationship described—or as if you're answering scoffers who have said that the Lord is *not* your shepherd—but certainly you would never stress "the."

Or take the first line of the Jones story "Lying Offshore," which appears in the resource section; "A ship rocked slowly upon the greasy seas." You might well stress "ship" and "seas," for a start. Further reflection might show the wisdom of stressing the verbal phrase "rocked slowly" to establish the mood. "Greasy," although a colorful adjective, could not be pointed over "seas," since ship and seas are the important ideas that must be established at the outset in presenting the story. And you would certainly subdue the words "a," "upon," and "the," since they do not carry the meaning.

2. Emphasize the new idea or the contrast, not the old idea. A pronoun, for example, is nearly always an old idea since it refers to someone or something already mentioned. Count on the listener's memory, and stress the new or contrasting ideas instead. For example:

And as they went <u>out</u> of Jericho, a great <u>crowd followed</u> him.[6]

"They" refers to Jesus and friends; "out" stresses their new direction. "Crowd" is the important new concept and must be given primary stress; "followed" may be stressed too, but if it is stressed heavily it may imply astonishment or the idea (by suggested contrast) that they had not followed him before that time.

Every sentence involves primary, secondary, and tertiary levels of stress, and your choice of words to stress will be guided by such questions as which words carry the ideas, which describe the essential action, and which convey newness or contrast.

3. Emphasize causal or conditional relationships. Sometimes these relationships are only implied, but in other passages they may be obvious. In the proverb "The fathers have eaten sour grapes,   and the children's teeth are set on edge,"[7] the causal relationship (because . . . therefore . . .) is implied. However, in the following sentence the conditional relationship (if . . . then . . .) is stated:

> And he said to all, "If any man would come after me, let him deny himself and take up his cross daily and follow me."[8]

Notice, in either case, how the significant words are stressed to bring out the causal or conditional relationship.

4. Emphasize the main thought rather than parenthetical phrases. Words don't have to be enclosed in parentheses to be considered parenthetical; unimportant phrases, asides, and tangential expressions may be thrown away (subdued, not stressed).

> George Bernard Shaw, as you well know, my friend, was a master of written and spoken English.

The phrase "as you well know, my friend" is parenthetical.

5. Finally, any word that can be omitted without significantly changing the meaning should not be stressed. In the sentence "The reader must live his ideas at the moment of utterance," the meaning is carried by *reader, live, ideas, moment, utterance,* and the other words may be read without stress. *Live, moment, utterance,* are the most important and should be stressed above *reader* (since in discussing the point it is probably assumed that we're talking about readers) and *ideas* (for that's probably an old idea by now).

In planning his interpretative strategy, the inexperienced reader might well mark up his lines to indicate stress and phrasing. You may or may not want to use a fully marked script for the performance. Some feel that doing so promotes a mechanical sort of reading. But it's useful to mark up your practice script. The virgule (slash) is used to show pause, with two slash marks for a long one; stress is shown by underlining. If you wish, you can use arrows to show the pitch direction for terminals. For example:

There was a time/ between the garden and the fiery furnace of self-destruct/ ⟍↘
between the nascent paradise and the burning tomb of nuclear detergent// ⟶ when man/ humble homo sapiens/ walked upon a world given him/ by One/ he would not recognize/ ⟍↘
That// was the time/ of man// [9] ⟍↘

Articulation and Projection

"The tip of the tongue, the lips, and the teeth" is a familiar classroom oral exercise. If you say it faster and faster, moving your tongue, lips, and teeth precisely to form each sound distinctly, you're going to improve your articulation (or enunciation, or diction, as it is sometimes called). Good *articulation* is important if you want to be heard and understood by your listeners, and it's also very rare in ordinary conversation today to hear a person speak precisely. Which means that your interpreters may have to work extra hard on this, for they are products of our slur-and-mumble culture. Tongue twisters are a good exercise (Peter Piper, etc.). You might run a whole rehearsal in which your readers are told they must over-enunciate everything, being very conscious of each sound that's uttered (cross your *t*'s vocally, you tell them) and producing it with extra effort. Pay special attention to the last consonant sounds (the "st" in *last* and the "nt" in *consonant*), for they are often dropped or mumbled by poor enunciators. And tell your readers to feel what their lips, teeth, and tongue are doing as they articulate various sounds. (If you make them a bit self-conscious it may help in the long run.) Also, have someone in the back of the room yell "Again!" whenever a reader's words have been slurred or indistinct.

Precise articulation means that half the *projection* battle is won too. Projection is a function of both loudness and articulation. When the Readers Theatre director yells, "Mary, I can't hear you back here—project!" he's saying several things, really: (1) "Speak louder, Mary," which means using more breath, or breathing more from the diaphragm to force more air through the vocal tract, or pausing more often to breathe instead of running out of breath in the attempt to sustain long phrases on a single breath. (2) "Speak more clearly, Mary," which refers to articulation but also means that she ought to slow down, probably, since it is generally when we hurry that we run sounds together and squash them. (3) "Talk to the back row, Mary," meaning that she must concentrate on reaching the people in the last row of seats. Projection includes all of this, maybe more.

The third point—talk to the back row—is a psychological matter. The reader must convince himself that every listener is important, even the people in the back, and he must remind himself that to speak to them requires a certain level of loudness. Too often readers forget the extent of their audience, particularly if the distant listeners are hidden in the shadows of the room. Speaking so loudly that it seems as if his voice is bouncing off the back wall is one way the reader can "psych" himself into an adequate projection.

With constant practice, readers may develop better breath control and more careful enunciation of sounds so that they can be heard easily without giving the appearance of shouting. By the way—recommend to your interpreters that they jog a mile a day! Any regular exercise that is strenuous enough to build lung power will help.

The Interpreter's Body

You speak with your whole body, not just your mouth. Your facial expression, stance or posture, and your gestures will assist your listeners in their effort to understand. Readers Theatre demands the development of an imaginary but strong visual scene. This requires a constant *aliveness* on the part of all readers in the scene. As Coger and White suggest,

> Since in Readers Theatre the characters move within a setting created in the minds of the audience, it is of paramount importance that the reader first create this scene in his own mind, that he see the characters in action within this mentally visualized setting. In so doing, he can appreciably aid the audience to re-create in *their* minds the scene, the characters, and the event.
> While the reader, as we have noted, thinks in terms of the traditional five senses—sight, sound, smell, touch, and taste—the senses of greatest importance to him as an interpreter are the kinetic and kinesthetic. The kinetic sense is an *overt* muscular response to the action inherent in the words. . . . Kinesthetic imagery calls for a *covert* muscular response to the emotion within the lines.[10]

If the reader is experiencing imaginatively the sensory stimuli in his lines—if he feels the pressure of the embrace, if he smells the acrid woodsmoke of the fire, if he sees the sun glaring on bronzed bodies at the beach, if he hears the ticktock of the family clock—he will respond not only vocally but physically to these images pounding through his consciousness. His muscular responses will be another means of involving the listener, vicariously if not directly.

Both covert and overt actions will result for an interpreter who's really in tune. Overtly he may shake his fist with Dr. Stockmann as he defies the entire village in *An Enemy of the People;* he may rise and stiffen with surprise as one of the prenatal souls reacting to the Butcher's appearance in *The Waiting Room,* or he may throw out his hands in a beckoning gesture as one of the friendly spirits in Lewis' *The Great Divorce.* The action of the moment may call for various facial expressions and/or bodily movement. The director will make specific suggestions if the readers fail to seize their opportunities or if their gestures seem inappropriate to the scene.

Covertly, also, the interpreter will be alive. Even if no broad movement is indicated, the reader's body will respond naturally to the mood of the passage. Demonstrate it to yourself. Sit before a mirror. Now read this line aloud, letting your muscles respond to the feelings in it: "She was a pleasant sight, standing on the greensward, about to approach my lawn chair with a pitcher of iced tea." Your muscles were probably quite relaxed. Now read this line: "Hurling myself into the surf, I swam with quick, sure strokes to the place where the shark had taken him under!" Didn't your muscles begin to tense, your posture change? Such a line almost pulls one off his seat! Even if you remain seated throughout, your posture—the way you recline or perch on your chair—will say something about your feeling, your character, the scene you're responding to! If you're fully involved and you let your body respond naturally as you read the lines, your physical response will help bring the literature to life for your listeners.

So the director, during rehearsals, must keep reminding his readers to "stay alive" when they're in the scene; even if they're not reading at the moment they should be looking at the focal point where the imaginary scene is taking place, and responding physically to what is happening. The director will have to warn other readers that they are stiff; they need to use their bodies more—to the extent that the mood and action of the scene is made visual as well as aural to the audience.

Now let me underline the importance of the reader's eyes. As we converse together we read each others' eyes, and often we learn how a person feels through his eyes, the so-called windows of the soul. The eyes are primary in facial expression; they reveal the character's feelings and attitudes as he speaks or reacts to others in the scene. So the reader must become very familiar with his lines. He should be able to take his eyes off the script for long moments, directing his gaze outward so that listeners can read his eyes and facial expression. Sometimes—often when he is the narrator—the reader will look directly at his auditors, but generally he will look at the imaginary scene over the heads of his listeners. In cases of onstage focus he will look at his fellow performers. In any case, he must get his nose out of his script book to be effective. A well-practiced interpreter shouldn't have to refer to his script more than once a sentence, briefly, if it's a medium-length sentence. Better readers may go for several sentences without referring to their books; much of the script is memorized.

During your solitary practice it may be helpful to read your lines aloud in front of a mirror. (You must practice them *aloud.*) Before a mirror, you see how you appear to your listeners at the moment of utterance. You can test your eye contact, try out gestures, note muscular response and facial expression.

Summing It Up: Identification, Visualization, Projection

We certainly can't deal with everything important to vocal and physical projection in one chapter. Readers who have particular problems in this area or need more details should consult one of the more comprehensive works on the subject of oral interpretation noted in the Bibliography. Some of them provide helpful exercises to improve your vocal abilities.

But I have tried to sketch the important considerations for you. Remember that whatever the reader does with his voice and body should enhance the meanings in the literature. That's his aim; he wants to help his listeners discover the meanings, get the message, and appreciate it, if not apply it. So the interpreter moves through the stages of identification, visualization, and projection.

I'm saying that the reader must first *identify* with the characters he is to suggest—and with the larger scene and the message of the literature he is reading. Secondly, he must *visualize* what is taking place so that he can help the audience to visualize it. By visualize I mean that he uses not only his eyes, but all of his senses to imaginatively feel and know the experience being described. Thirdly, the reader *projects* that experience to his audience, fully utilizing his vocal and physical resources. If the team effort is effective, the listener too will identify because he is able to visualize.

When this happens, minds are stirred and stretched and miracles may happen, as that which was merely ink and parchment now takes on the radiance of reality. All of this happens when the team of interpreters becomes a bridge between the parchment and the people.

Staging Readers Theatre

Simplicity and imagination are the keys to Readers Theatre. The very simplicity of its staging forces the listener to use his imagination. So you may have a number of readers holding manuscripts, standing on a bare platform with neither costumes nor scenery to back them—and it may be a very powerful experience! Although you may find that simple costumes or fragmentary scenery or lighting changes are useful, none of it is essential. Very little stage movement is employed. Obviously Readers Theatre lends itself to the church chancel where movement is restricted and where elaborate properties and scenery seem incongruous.

Types of Focus

Focus refers to the gaze of the interpreter. When he lifts his eyes from his book, where does he look? You need to reach an agreement on this with your cast in order to be consistent. There are some artistic matters that you need to think about in making a decision on focus. Basically, readers can employ three kinds of focus—but probably not all three in the same performance!

The first may be termed *narrative* focus, since the narrator, if there is one, would use it to convey his description to the audience. He would look directly into the eyes of his listeners, picking out one here, one there, and so on. If a reader other than the narrator becomes the storyteller momentarily (that is, he is not speaking as a character in the scene), he might use narrative focus also. Eye contact with members of the audience will involve them, draw them in, make them part of the story. Narrative sections may be read directly to the audience, while offstage or onstage focus is employed for the dramatic material.

For the dramatic sections—actual dialogue between characters in the imaginary scene—you have your choice of offstage or onstage focus. Many argue that *offstage* focus is more appropriate to the style of Readers Theatre. Using offstage focus, readers direct their gaze at some imaginary scene visualized somewhere over the audience, and they react to that scene as if they can see themselves suspended in a large mirror hung on the back wall and just above the level of the audience. (The mirror concept is a good way to orient your cast and help them try out offstage focus.) So the readers look out and up rather than at each other, which psychologically takes the action away from the stage and puts it into the auditors' minds.

This makes sense, doesn't it? No one's going to believe that the action is taking place onstage anyway, so why not pretend it's going on inside people's heads? If your readers focus offstage, their sight lines would converge at some point above the audience and about halfway to the back wall, as in figure 1.

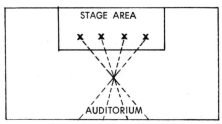

FIGURE 1. OFFSTAGE FOCUS

Theoretically the gaze of individual readers would vary, depending on whom they were addressing in the "mirror"; in practice, this is seldom reduced to a science.

The main problem with offstage focus is that your readers may complain, "It's unnatural. I'm addressing that character now, so why shouldn't I look at him?" The statement ignores the fact that the "character" is not the same as the person reading the lines; the reader is onstage, to be sure, but the character is imagined and part of an imaginary scene "out there," not onstage. But you will have trouble explaining that to some readers. Consequently it's occasionally necessary to give in to cast pressure and permit *onstage* focus.

Onstage focus means simply that the readers look at each other while reading. It's probably better for certain kinds of material, and it does seem more natural to the readers. (But don't always do the easiest thing. Sometimes the most artistic way is the least comfortable.) Sometimes you may want to switch from offstage to onstage focus when a climax is reached because the change may highlight the struggle or point of crisis.

The type of material makes a difference. A formal, heavier piece such as a verse drama may lend itself more to offstage focus; a lighter, satirical piece might better fit the casual spirit of onstage focus. Even more determinant are the factors of size of cast and the type of staging envisioned. A large-cast reading is probably better with offstage focus than, say, a reading by two or three interpreters. In the large-cast reading, the levels and spacing of readers (assuming they remain fixed throughout) makes it virtually impossible to employ onstage focus. Downstage readers would have their backs turned to the readers upstage (away from the audience), who might also be elevated. For the downstage people to look at the upstage people would take some fancy neck swiveling! Of course, if you block movements for your readers from one scene to the next you may eliminate this problem.

How to make physical action credible is a severe headache connected with offstage focus. Granted, readers won't move around much or come to blows on stage, but physical action or violence may be part of the story. Staging it is difficult with both kinds of focus, but harder with offstage. In staging a reading of *The Gardener Who Was Afraid of Death*, we pondered how to stage the murder of Phocus by the Roman soldier at the play's end. We used offstage focus throughout, so the readers never confronted each other; Phocus sat center stage with the two soldiers on either side, all facing out. We decided to suggest the killing this way: At the critical moment the soldier simply raised his arm and brought it down (holding an imaginary sword) in a frontal gesture; Phocus buckled and sank to his knees. When the movements were carefully synchronized it looked artistic. Actually, Phocus could have just dropped his head and it would still have worked—in fact, it might have been more suggestive. Since offstage focus was used throughout, it seemed natural to finish the play in that style. However, one could make a case for a switch to onstage focus at the climactic moment.

On the other hand, in staging a reading of Ralph Stone's *Construction*,[1] I used onstage focus throughout with the ending done in stylized movement. The readers maintained fixed positions on stage, sitting or standing, but they looked at each other. The violence was suggested in different ways. Where the script has a fight between Art, the policeman, and Terry, the teen-ager, the two readers stepped off their respective platforms and took a step to confront each other near center stage. Other confrontations were suggested by vocal changes, stance, and the jumping up or turning of readers rather than by more realistic action. At the very end of the play, when the Builder is hung on a cross, the readers dropped their books and moved into a stylized mob-attack sequence, broken by blackouts and timed to the sharp incessant beat of wooden drumsticks hit against each other, culminating with the final "still" showing the man on the cross and the reactions of the others to what they had done. There was a single spot on center stage where the figure stood with his arms held out symbolically (no cross was actually used). All of this was suggestive, not realistic, and had a strong impact on the audience. *Construction,* with its ten volatile characters and violent action, is not an easy play to adapt for Readers Theatre.

Staging Readers Theatre may well hinge upon the director's choice of offstage or onstage focus. Once this basic decision is made, other problems come unsnarled.

Positioning the Readers

One problem is positioning. The stool is the reader's basic prop. Groups which do a lot of Readers Theatre may buy their stools in various sizes. Stools are portable, take up very little space, and permit the reader to turn sideways or even to turn his back on the audience very easily, without standing. Of course, stools with swivel seats are dandy! But if stools are not available, interpreters can sit on other kinds of furniture—chairs, benches, boxes, stumps, ladders, even scaffolding. In some productions you may prefer to have your readers stand, with or without lecterns.

What about lecterns? Their advantage is that once your reading script is on the lectern your hands are free to gesture. This makes for more alive readers, some say. On the other hand, the lectern hides a part of the reader so that he's not completely visible. A music stand with the typical thin rod provides good visibility and is a fine tool, provided you don't lean too heavily on it!

A major objection to the lectern is that it becomes a barrier between reader and listener. A forest of reading stands on stage may look like a set of bars interposed between the reading team and its audience. Readers Theatre demands a psychological intimacy which might be endangered. Personally, I prefer doing without lecterns. My readers usually hold their manuscripts in one hand, gesture with the other, and are completely visible to the audience. I don't close my mind to the use of lecterns, however. In doing a college production of Stephen Leacock's story "Behind the Beyond,"[2] I had my readers stand behind lecterns when in the scene, and their formal stance enhanced the humor of the piece. Combined with offstage focus and a declamatory thespian style, the whole effect was wonderfully ludicrous.

Use of Stage Space

Both the vertical and horizontal spacing of readers is possible—spacing them on different levels and at various distances across the stage area, left to right. Spacing in depth, however, is not particularly important unless the audience is seated on a higher plane than the readers and has a sort of bird's-eye view. Your grouping of people on stage functions to (1) provide an artistically satisfying visual effect for the audience, and (2) suggest the relationships or imply the relative importance of the characters. The larger the cast, the better it is to break up the space into some viable visual configuration.

Various levels or heights are especially helpful with a large-cast reading. You can build and arrange platforms or use stools of various heights, or you can use ladders, scaffolding, or steps. The divided chancel offers good staging possibilities, for it usually has center steps where readers can stand on different levels. Using different heights makes the stage picture aesthetically interesting and may also suggest the relative importance of characters. You could set off the narrator, for example, by placing him above the other readers, or you could put the protagonist, hero, or king above the others. You may have good reason to put certain readers below the others, as well. In staging a reading of the trial scene from Shaw's *Saint Joan*, I put the Inquisitor and Bishop Cauchon on the highest of three levels and seated the heroine, Joan of Arc, directly downstage and on a bench, much below them. The other characters were seated on the two side platforms at an intermediate height. (See figure 2.) This arrangement seemed to symbolize the various levels of temporal and spiritual authority being represented.

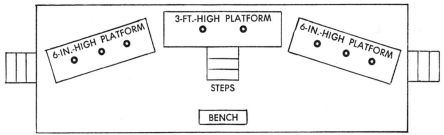

FIGURE 2. STAGING FOR TRIAL SCENE, *Saint Joan*

Consider your horizontal spacing, too. You may want to have the readers who speak to each other more sit together; or, to bring out hostility or conflict between two characters in the story, you might seat those readers at the extreme left and right of the stage. (This would work better with offstage focus, of course.) If you have a line of readers across the stage, you may want to alternate men and women, avoid putting all the tall people at one end, or in other ways try to develop the best possible stage picture. Much of this is a matter of taste, so I'm not going to be highly prescriptive. And as we apply our guidelines to specific cases, we find there's no one right way. We're left with lots of options.

Take the simplest possible setting, a two-person dialogue reading like the scene involving Hank Gavin and a bartender in the St. Johns novel *Tell No Man.* Gavin is a young businessman (about to turn minister) who is questioning the local bartender about his religious views. What are the options for staging? First, you might try staging it with the two readers standing or sitting side by side—could be effective with skilled interpreters, but it's not too imaginative. So you try using different levels: one reader stands on a platform, or one is sitting while the other stands. We did it in the church chancel with Gavin seated on a stool and the bartender standing nearby with a towel draped symbolically over one arm. Simplicity and imagination!

Or, take Warren Kliewer's *Sacrifice to Virtue,* appearing in the drama anthology *What Are We Going to Do with All These Rotting Fish?*[3] A pastor is counseling a teen-ager who tells him of her recent sexual experience. The pastor condemns her until he discovers that the boy in question is his own son; then he has to rethink his position. The scene could be staged with the pastor standing behind the girl. Since her back would be to him, offstage focus would be used. (Incidentally, offstage focus enhances listener comprehension since faces are front and voices are more audible.) This arrangement would suggest the idea of a bewildered, not-quite-penitent young lady sitting before the authority figure for counsel. It's not the only way to stage it but it makes sense. With *x* to represent a standing reader and *o* for a seated one, figure 3 is our diagram for *Sacrifice to Virtue.*

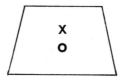

FIGURE 3. VERTICAL STAGING FOR *Sacrifice to Virtue*

Now let's look at a piece for three readers. What are the options for staging something like O. Henry's "The Gift of the Magi" or Dietz's *Old Ymir's Clay Pot?* In both, the readers are employed as narrators of the story as well as characters in it. The O. Henry tale is included in this book. The Dietz fable, from his book *Fables & Vaudevilles & Plays,* is a delightfully haunting parable-poem for three voices. Figure 4 shows some options for arranging the three readers, using steps, a raised platform, or stools of differing heights.

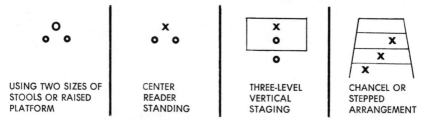

FIGURE 4. FOUR WAYS OF STAGING *Old Ymir's Clay Pot*

I have staged *Old Ymir's Clay Pot* two ways, as in the first and third frames of figure 4. My wife prefers the vertical arrangement as in the third frame because, she says, the audience can hold all three readers in view more easily. It's the difference between watching a pitcher throw a baseball from a seat behind third base and from an elevated position behind home plate. It's easier to keep pitcher, catcher, hitter, and umpire in view together from behind home plate—and much easier to follow the pitch and see it curve!

If your chancel has center steps it makes staging easier. In doing the scene from Ibsen that's included in the resource section, I put the four readers on the chancel steps using offstage focus. It made a neat little group (see figure 5).

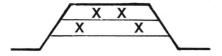

FIGURE 5. CHANCEL STAGING FOR SCENE FROM *An Enemy of the People*

If steps are not available, use something else to provide different heights. My play *The Waiting Room* can be read effectively with all the readers seated on a flat stage, but with the four prenatal souls downstage on low chairs while the upstage two read from high stools, as in figure 6.

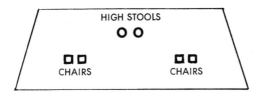

FIGURE 6. STAGING FOR *The Waiting Room*

Offstage focus was used throughout the performance. Stools are needed only for the readers upstage, the Angel and the Butcher, who need to turn to make entrances and exits—they can just spin and turn front or back to the audience. The front four remain in the scene throughout and can be seated on chairs.

The Cookie Tree is a delightful children's story with some Christian

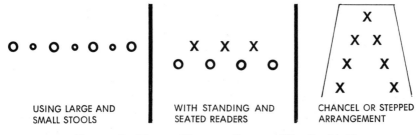

FIGURE 7. THREE WAYS OF STAGING *The Cookie Tree*

implications. The cast is flexible, since the characters can easily be doubled or tripled. Figure 7 shows three ways of staging *The Cookie Tree* for seven readers. No doubt you can think of others.

In staging *The Great Divorce* as Readers Theatre (note the excerpt of it included in the resource section), I felt that the key figures were the narrator (Lewis, the storyteller) and George Macdonald (his spiritual mentor), so I elevated these readers upstage. Then I staggered six chairs left and right to accommodate the other interpreters, with each of them reading more than one character. The story is largely a series of conversations between pairs of characters; to help the audience understand, I put a bench down center and had the pairs of readers move to that bench for their particular dialogues at the right time. We maintained offstage focus, however. When a conversation was finished, the two interpreters returned to their original seats. (See figure 8.)

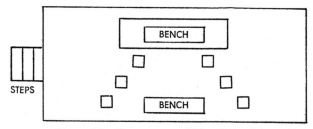

FIGURE 8. STAGING FOR *The Great Divorce*

If you add more readers you complicate the staging more. In their manual on Readers Theatre, Coger and White include the diagram (figure 9) and description of an adaptation of the book of Job which are reprinted here for illustration. This will give you an idea of the complexity of large-cast staging.

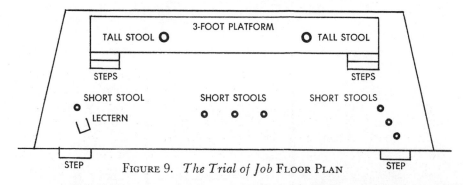

FIGURE 9. *The Trial of Job* FLOOR PLAN

This Master of Arts thesis-project was based primarily on the Book of Job but included additional material drawn from other books of the Bible. The faculty cast of ten included, in addition to the narrator, readers who interpreted the roles of God, Job, Satan, Eliphaz, Bildad, Zophar, and Three Messengers. The physical arrangement was simple. A long, narrow, three-foot high platform with a tall stool at either end occupied most of the upstage playing space. There were three shorter stools at DC, three more arranged at an angle at L and DL, and a short stool and a lectern at DR. The tall stool on the platform at UR was for God; the one at UL, for Satan. Eliphaz, Bildad, and Zophar were seated on the stools DC, the Three Messengers on the three stools at L and DL, and the narrator on a stool at DR. No one stood except the narrator, who rose and took his position at the lectern when he was required to advance the story.

Primarily, the focus was offstage; however, God and Satan—although they did not look at each other—did look down on the human beings, observed them, and listened to them. Because the auditorium was not equipped with a front curtain and had no backstage area, the readers sat in the front row of the auditorium until the presentation was to begin; they then rose, walked sedately up the steps to the stage, and took their seats. All except Satan were dressed somberly in black suits, white shirts, and dark ties; Satan sported a red tie and a red pocket handkerchief.[4]

Staging Readers Theatre in the round poses some problems. Offstage focus is unlikely, but it may be possible to keep the reading team together as one wedge of the circle with the audience composing the rest of it. In one case, we read a scene from around the piano, appropriately the wedding from *Our Town*, with a pianist-reader playing a few bars of music as a lead-in to the wedding. (See figure 10.)

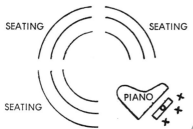

Figure 10.
ARENA STAGING FOR SCENE FROM *Our Town*

Sometimes you can position your readers facing each other across the circle. If they have strong voices or the room is not very large, it may work well. We staged a unit of two scenes from my biographical play about Martin Niemoeller in this way. The initial scene found Pastor Niemoeller talking to his church secretary in preparation for an important meeting at Hitler's chancery; the second scene was that confrontation with Adolf Hitler at which also Herr Goering appeared. We read the first one from the nine o'clock position of the circle, with the secretary seated and Niemoeller standing. We did the second scene with Niemoeller moving to the six o'clock position, and Hitler and Goering at twelve and three o'clock. The three readers stood still but glared at each other across the distance. In this way the dramatic climax was reached, and listeners responded well to the presentation. (See figure 11.)

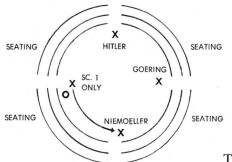

FIGURE 11.   ARENA STAGING FOR
TWO SCENES FROM *God Is My Fuehrer*

You can have your readers move around if you wish—to make transitions between scenes or to mark an important climax—but keep in mind that if stage blocking becomes very detailed, simplicity and suggestion are no longer the tools that unlock the imagination. Enough said about positioning your readers. Attempt—experiment—improvise!

Making Entrances and Exits

How do you get your characters into and out of the scene? Various options are possible. If readers are to stand throughout, then to seat a character might take him out of the scene. Having him turn his back may be better. He does not have to leave the stage! When readers are seated on stools, turning the back seems to be the best way to exit. Lacking stools, it's possible for the interpreter to drop his head to show that he's left the scene, provided the gesture is definite and is done that way consistently so that the audience gets the point. At the end of the performance I have my readers close their books to indicate termination. (At this point the audience knows it's time to applaud, throw things, escape through the vestibule, or prepare for the offering!)

Lighting changes may be another way to indicate transitions or show termination. If your lighting system is sophisticated you can raise or dim spots on stage areas to include or exclude particular readers. This will move readers in or out of the scene quite simply!

Candlelighting may also be effective on occasion. I used it once with a reading of Kennedy's *The Terrible Meek* given by young people at a Senior High Conference. This is a moving drama involving conversations that take place at the foot of the cross following the death of Jesus— including his mother, Mary, and two Roman soldiers. It was written to be played in darkness. I put my three readers behind a low table with candles in front of them. When a reader entered the scene he lighted his candle; when he left, he blew it out. Eventually I want to try some other readings by candlelight, including my play *The Way Station*. Material with a mysterious mood, which deals with mysterious subjects like the afterlife, or which is set at night would lend itself to presentation by candlelight.

Technical Effects

What about costumes, lighting, sound effects, and scenery—the trappings of the conventional stage? I think I've made my point that in Readers Theatre they're not essential—and may be detrimental. But there are times when you're intrigued by the use of special effects which may enhance the meaning.

As to costumes, again the keynote is simplicity. But keep in mind that dressing your readers a particular way may be helpful. Having them all dressed alike may show that it's a *team* effort, and suggest unity. Or some of the characters may be dressed alike. In doing *The Waiting Room* I had the four prenatal souls wear identical black and blue outfits, but I dressed the Butcher in an open-collared white shirt with khaki trousers. (We decided against putting a butcher's apron on him, replete with bloodstains!) The Angel wore a white dress with a black decorative pattern. So we had a uniform appearance for the prenatal souls with variations for the other two characters to suggest their roles better.

It's easier to use costumes to suggest character when the reader assumes only one role during the performance. If he assumes several roles it will be impossible to change costume each time, although he might add just a touch of something—a handkerchief, a cap, a turning up of the collar —to indicate that he's now a different personality. But you may want to convey the uniform look by having your readers all dress alike. One director staged Henry Fielding's amusing play *The Tragedy of Tragedies; or, The Life and Death of Tom Thumb the Great* with everyone wearing formal evening attire; the attire added to the spirit of burlesque in the comedy. Again, personal preference, the material itself, and the occasion are your guides—not a set of formal rules. You could stage a reading of Robert Sherwood's *Abe Lincoln in Illinois* with everyone in period costuming. Or, to downplay the realism and stimulate the imagination—or to make it seem more contemporary—you could do it in modern dress. If possible, do it both ways and compare!

Audiovisual effects may help you at times. We used some drumming to help build to a climax during a reading of the martyrdom of Thomas More. Excerpts from Saint-Saëns's *Carnival of the Animals* provide appropriate transitions for reading *Animal Farm*, Orwell's fable about totalitarianism. And a reading of *God Is My Fuehrer* may be punctuated with Beethoven music, battle sounds, an American march, the noise of marching feet, cheering crowds, a whistled hymn.

Some directors have experimented with slide projections of visual symbols or pictures during a reading. Again, you need to be sure that the visual does not detract from the aural element, since it is to be a reading and not a slide show. There will be times when slides or visual stimuli will help and times when they will confuse. The same is true of using pantomimed action during a reading. I remember seeing a televised performance of Dylan Thomas' *Under Milk Wood* in which several performers pantomimed action appropriate to the narrative as it was spoken by others. It was very well done. Of course, you could take slide pictures of the pantomimed action and show them, but the live pantomime would be better. However, you might want to use pantomime during breaks in the reading rather than during the reading itself.

A final word about lighting and scenery. Three guidelines apply: Keep it simple. Use your imagination. Work with what you have. Lighting is great if you have a dimmer system with floods and spots that can illuminate certain stage areas; otherwise you just flick some wall switches and let your readers carry the ball. As for scenery—other than platforms, railings, and the like, scenery is seldom used for Readers Theatre. Usually it's presented against a neutral background like the chancel wall or a black curtain. Conceivably you could erect a silhouette tree or outline one on the backdrop for a reading of *The Cookie Tree* or display a Christian flag and a Nazi swastika overhead with a reading of *God Is My Fuehrer*. Suggestive fragmentary scenery may enhance the meanings without subverting the message. But the rule is: When in doubt, do without! Let the readers carry the ball. Bare stage and neutral background is still your best bet for Readers Theatre.

I've said all this not to give you a set of rules but to suggest guidelines for your experimentation, based on my experience and that of others. So . . . attempt . . . risk . . . experiment . . . and enjoy! It is possible, after all, for group reading to be fun even if it's also worship.

Readers Theatre
Comes to Church

RESOURCES

Here are eleven sample scripts, adapted for Readers Theatre, each with a brief introduction. I have used most of these materials in performance, and I intend to use the others. Several have been worship ingredients. In every case except for "Where Have All the Flowers Gone?" the adaptation is my own. In some cases you may decide to modify or revise these adaptations. No matter; at least you have an idea of what may be done.

These pieces represent various types of literature: plays, poetry, a novel, a newspaper column, several short stories of various descriptions, the Bible. Some are old favorites, others are new creations. They are for small casts, many of them for just two or three readers, and will not present much difficulty in staging.

You must not assume that any published or copyrighted material may be performed publicly without express permission from the copyright holder or publisher. If in doubt about whether a particular performance is "public" rather than for a private, limited group, write to the publisher of the material for guidance.

Shadrach, Meshach, and Abednego
from Daniel 3

With its majestic line, its rhythm, repetition, and imagery, this Old Testament story is sheer poetry. And it carries a timeless message of men of faith who refused to compromise under fire! This adaptation of Daniel 3 is choric speech, to be sure; also, broadly defined, it's Readers Theatre. Although the four VOICES function in concert as storyteller, individual readers are assigned particular characters to interpret. Vocal effects are introduced to help make the lines live imaginatively for the audience and to bring out the poetic qualities of the literature. (Experiment with male and female voices to see which works best.) Contrast this adaptation with the script for "The Man Born Blind" following; this one leaves the Biblical wording virtually unchanged and makes use of special vocal effects, while the adaptation of John 9 involves much more paraphrasing to modernize some of the language, along with some inserted exclamations to create a more realistic crowd effect. Also, the latter doesn't use echo effects or unison lines. The two stories are different kinds of literature and must be treated differently.

VOICE 1. King Nebuchadnezzar made an image of gold, whose height was sixty cubits and its breadth six cubits. He set it up on the plain of Dura, in the province of Babylon.

VOICE 2. Then King Nebuchadnezzar sent to assemble the satraps, the prefects, and the governors, the counselors, the treasurers, the justices, the magistrates, and all the officials of the provinces to come to the dedication of the image which King Nebuchadnezzar had set up.

VOICE 3. Then the satraps, the prefects, and the governors, the counselors, the treasurers, the justices, the magistrates, and all the officials of the provinces, were assembled for the dedication of the image that King Nebuchadnezzar had set up; and they stood before the image that King Nebuchadnezzar had set up.

VOICE 4. And the herald proclaimed aloud,

VOICE 1. *(As if to a multitude.)* You are commanded, O peoples, nations, and languages, that when you hear the sound of the horn

VOICE 4. horn   *(Echo*

VOICE 1. pipe   *effect.)*

VOICE 4. pipe

VOICE 1. lyre

VOICE 4. lyre

VOICE 1. trigon

VOICE 4. trigon

VOICE 1. harp

VOICE 4. harp

VOICE 1. bagpipe

VOICE 4. bagpipe

ALL. and every kind of music,

VOICE 1. you are to fall down and worship

VOICE 2. worship   *(Echo,*

VOICE 3. worship   *fading.)*

VOICE 4. worship

VOICE 1. worship the golden image that King Nebuchadnezzar has set up; and whoever does not fall down and worship shall be cast into a burning

OTHERS. burning   *(Increasing*

VOICE 1. fiery   *in intensity*

OTHERS. fiery   *each time.)*

VOICE 1. furnace.

OTHERS. furnace.

VOICE 4. Therefore, as soon as all the peoples heard the sound of the horn, pipe, lyre, trigon, harp, bagpipe, and every kind of music, all the peoples, nations, and languages fell down and worshiped the golden image which King Nebuchadnezzar had set up.

VOICE 1. Therefore at that time certain Chaldeans came forward and maliciously accused the Jews. They said to King Nebuchadnezzar,

OTHERS. O King, live for ever!

VOICE 2. *(Oily manner.)* You, O King, have made a decree, that every man who hears the sound of the horn, pipe, lyre, trigon, harp, bagpipe, and every kind of music

VOICE 3. *(Similar tone.)* shall fall down and worship the golden image;

VOICE 4. *(Very sinister.)* and whoever does not fall down and worship shall be cast into a burning

VOICE 1. And the satraps, the prefects, the governors, and the king's counselors gathered together and saw that the fire had not had any power over the bodies of those men; the hair of their heads was not singed, their mantles were not harmed, and no smell of fire had come upon them. Nebuchadnezzar said,

VOICE 3. Blessed be the God of Shadrach, Meshach, and Abednego, who has sent his angel and delivered his servants, who trusted in him, and set at nought the king's command, and yielded up their bodies rather than serve any god except their own God. Therefore I make a decree: Any people, nation, or language

OTHERS. Any people, nation, or language   *(Chanted repetition*

VOICE 3. that speaks anything against the God   *for effect.)*

OTHERS. that speaks anything against the God

VOICE 3. of Shadrach, Meshach, and Abednego

OTHERS. of Shadrach, Meshach, and Abednego

VOICE 3. shall be torn limb from limb,

OTHERS. shall be torn limb from limb,

VOICE 3. and their houses laid in ruins;   *(Stronger,*

OTHERS. and their houses laid in ruins;   *louder.)*

VOICE 3. *(Pause. Slower, wondering.)* for there is no other god who is able to deliver in this way.

VOICE 1. Then the king promoted Shadrach, Meshach, and Abednego in the province of Babylon.

The Man Born Blind
from John 9

This is an adaptation of the story in John 9 of the man born blind. I have followed the original outline of the story and retained much of the dialogue, but I have modernized some of the language, deleted a few unnecessary lines, and written some additional remarks to help the audience imagine crowds of people. Although edited for four male readers (JESUS, MAN 1, MAN 2, MAN 3) and two females (the WOMAN and the NARRATOR), the cast might be cut by one or two persons if necessary. This illustrates what may be done with Gospel material; a program of cuttings from John or the presentation of an entire Gospel by a reading team could be a stirring event for the Christian community.

NARRATOR. As Jesus walked along, he saw a man born blind. His disciples were curious about the man.

MAN 1. Teacher, who sinned—this man or his parents—that he was born blind?

JESUS. Friends, blindness is not a punishment. He was not born blind because of sin—either his sin or his parents'—but that God's work might be demonstrated. We must do the works of the Father now, while it is still daylight—soon the night will come, when no one can work. As long as I am here with you, I am the light of the world.

NARRATOR. Having said this, Jesus spat on the ground (*the person reading Jesus could simulate this*) and took the spittle and made clay. Then he annointed the man's eyes with the clay.

JESUS. Go and wash in the pool of Siloam.

NARRATOR. So he went off and washed his eyes and—(*with a tone of awe*) came back—seeing! The man's neighbors and acquaintances were astonished.

MAN 2. Isn't this the blind beggar?

MAN 1. Well, this man's not blind!

WOMAN. It can't be the same man!

MAN 1. It looks like the same man!

MAN 2. Sure, he used to sit right there and beg alms!

WOMAN. I tell you, it's not the man!

MAN 2. And I say it is!

MAN 3. *(Pause.)* I am the man.

MAN 1. Oh, yeah?

WOMAN. But now you can see. How come?

MAN 3. The man called Jesus made some clay and put it on my eyes, and he told me to wash in the pool of Siloam . . . So I went and I washed . . . And now I can see!

MAN 2. Huh. *(A moment of bewilderment.)* Well, where is he?

WOMAN. Yes, where is he now—this man called Jesus?

MAN 3. I don't know.

NARRATOR. So they took the man to the Pharisees. Keep in mind that it was the Sabbath Day when Jesus healed him. The Pharisees began to interrogate the poor fellow.

MAN 1. How did you get your sight, man?

MAN 3. He put clay on my eyes—

MAN 1. Who did? Speak up!

MAN 3. Jesus. And—I washed my eyes, and now I can see!

MAN 2. This man Jesus is not from God. He doesn't observe the Sabbath!

MAN 1. Who knows? He has done marvelous works. They are signs which may—

MAN 2. Nonsense. How can a sinful man do such things?

MAN 1. Well, sir, what do you say about this man who has opened your eyes?

MAN 3. He is a prophet.

NARRATOR. The Jews did not believe that he had been blind, and had received his sight, so they called in the man's parents.

MAN 1. Is this your son? Was he born blind? How can he see?

WOMAN. *(With great deference.)* We know that . . . this is our son and . . . he was born blind. But we don't know what happened to him, and we don't know who opened his eyes. Ask him, gentlemen—he is of age and he can speak for himself.

NARRATOR. So for the second time they called him in and questioned him.

MAN 2. Give God the praise; we know that Jesus is a sinner!

MAN 3. I don't know whether he is a sinner or not; one thing I do know, that although I was blind, now I see.

MAN 2. What did he do to you? How did he open your eyes?

MAN 3. I have told you already, and you wouldn't listen. Why do you want to hear it again? Do you too wish to become his disciples?

Together, overlapping, angrily:
   MAN 2. What! Nonsense, man! Do you dare insult us?
   MAN 1. Stupid ass! Nobody in his right mind— Peasant! Blasphemer!

MAN 2. You may be his disciple, but we are disciples of Moses! God has spoken to Moses, but as for this man, he's got no credentials!
MAN 3. Well, that is strange. You don't accept this man Jesus, and yet he cured my blindness. Never since the world began has anyone healed a man born blind. If this were not God's man, he could do nothing.

Together, overlapping, angrily:
   MAN 2. Incredible nonsense! Shut your mouth, you!
   MAN 1. Sinner! Blasphemer! Stupid disciple of a fool!

MAN 2. You were born in utter sin! Do you expect to teach us anything?
NARRATOR. And they threw him out . . . Now Jesus heard that they had thrown him out, and he returned to see him.
JESUS. Do you believe in the Son of Man?
MAN 3. And who is he, sir, that I may believe in him?
JESUS. He is speaking to you now.
MAN 3. Oh yes! I do believe!
JESUS. I have come into this world as a judge, so that those who do not see may see, and those who see may become blind.
NARRATOR. Some of the Pharisees near him heard this, and they were insulted.
MAN 1. *(Derisively loud.)* Are we too blind?
JESUS. *(With steady assurance.)* If you were blind, you would not be guilty; but since you think that you can see, your guilt is certain.

The Gift of the Magi
from the story by O. Henry

This famous O. Henry short story speaks to the universal theme of love—even the sacrifice of a lesser love to a greater love. Its marvelous ironic twist and poignant sentiment can touch even the hearts of moderns with their smug sophistication—and not only at Christmas, although it is a Christmas story. Read it with offstage or onstage focus, arrange your readers in vertical or horizontal space style, do it for Sunday morning worship or at a family Christmas program—that doesn't really matter. What does matter is that it be interpreted skillfully by persons who can capture the beautiful sweet-sadness of the story. Three readers are needed: the NARRATOR, DELLA, and JIM.

NARRATOR. One dollar and eighty-seven cents. That was all. And sixty cents of it was in pennies. Pennies saved one and two at a time by bulldozing the grocer and the vegetable man and the butcher until one's cheeks burned with the silent imputation of parsimony that such close dealing implied.

DELLA. Three times Della counted it. One dollar and eighty-seven cents. And the next day would be Christmas. There was clearly nothing to do but flop down on the shabby little couch and howl. So Della did it.

NARRATOR. Which instigates the moral reflection that life is made up of sobs, sniffles, and smiles, with sniffles predominating.

JIM. While the mistress of the house is gradually subsiding from the first stage to the second, take a look at the home. A furnished flat at $8 per week. It did not exactly beggar description, but it certainly had that word on the lookout for the mendicancy squad.

In the vestibule below was a letter-box into which no letter would go, and an electric button from which no mortal finger could coax a ring. Also appertaining thereunto was a card bearing the name "Mr. James Dillingham Young."

NARRATOR. The "Dillingham" had been flung to the breeze during a former period of prosperity when its possessor was being paid $30 per week. Now, when the income was shrunk to $20, the letters of "Dillingham" looked blurred, as though they were thinking seriously of contracting to a modest and unassuming D. But whenever Mr. James Dillingham Young came home and reached his flat above he was called "Jim" and greatly hugged by Mrs. James Dillingham Young, already introduced to you as Della. Which is all very good.

DELLA. Della finished her cry and attended to her cheeks with the powder rag. She stood by the window and looked out dully at a gray cat walking a gray fence in a gray backyard. Tomorrow would be Christmas Day, and she had only $1.87 with which to buy Jim a present. She had been saving every penny she could for months, with this result. Twenty dollars a week doesn't go far. Expenses had been greater than she had calculated. They always are. Only $1.87 to buy a present for Jim. Her Jim. Many a happy hour she had spent planning for something nice for him. Something fine and rare and sterling—something just a little bit near to being worthy of the honor of being owned by Jim.

JIM. There was a pier-glass between the windows of the room. Perhaps you have seen a pier-glass in an $8 flat. A very thin and very agile person may, by observing his reflection in a rapid sequence of longitudinal strips, obtain a fairly accurate conception of his looks. Della, being slender, had mastered the art.

DELLA. Suddenly she whirled from the window and stood before the glass. Her eyes were shining brilliantly, but her face had lost its color within twenty seconds. Rapidly she pulled down her hair and let it fall its full length.

NARRATOR. Now, there were two possessions of the James Dillingham Youngs in which they both took a mighty pride. One was Jim's gold watch that had been his father's and his grandfather's. The other was Della's hair. Had the Queen of Sheba lived in the flat across the airshaft, Della would have let her hair hang out the window some day to dry just to depreciate Her Majesty's jewels and gifts. Had King Solomon been the janitor, with all his treasures piled up in the basement, Jim would have pulled out his watch every time he passed, just to see him pluck at his beard from envy.

DELLA. So now Della's beautiful hair fell about her rippling and shining like a cascade of brown waters. It reached below her knee and made itself almost a garment for her. And then she did it up again nervously and quickly. Once she faltered for a minute and stood still while a tear or two splashed on the worn red carpet.

NARRATOR. On went her old brown jacket; on went her old brown hat. With a whirl of skirts and with the brilliant sparkle still in her eyes, she fluttered out the door and down the stairs to the street.

Where she stopped the sign read: "Mme. Sofronie. Hair Goods of All Kinds." One flight up Della ran, and collected herself, panting. Madame, large, too white, chilly, hardly looked the "Sofronie."

DELLA. "Will you buy my hair?"

NARRATOR. "I buy hair. Take yer hat off and let's have a sight at the looks of it," said Madame. Down rippled the brown cascade. "Twenty dollars," said Madame, lifting the mass with a practised hand.

DELLA. "Give it to me quick!"

NARRATOR. Oh, and the next two hours tripped by on rosy wings. Forget the hashed metaphor. She was ransacking the stores for Jim's present.

JIM. She found it at last. It surely had been made for Jim and no one else. There was no other like it in any of the stores, and she had turned all of them inside out. It was a platinum fob chain simple and chaste in design, properly proclaiming its value by substance alone and not by meretricious ornamentation—as all good things should do. It was even worthy of The Watch.

DELLA. As soon as she saw it she knew that it must be Jim's. It was like him. Quietness and value—the description applied to both. Twenty-one dollars they took from her for it, and she hurried home with the 87 cents. With that chain on his watch Jim might be properly anxious about the time in any company. Grand as the watch was, he sometimes looked at it on the sly on account of the old leather strap that he used in place of a chain.

NARRATOR. When Della reached home her intoxication gave way a little to prudence and reason. She got out her curling irons and lighted the gas and went to work repairing the ravages made by generosity added to love. Which is always a tremendous task, dear friends—a mammoth task.

Within forty minutes her head was covered with tiny, close-lying curls that made her look wonderfully like a truant schoolboy. She looked at her reflection in the mirror long, carefully, and critically.

DELLA. "If Jim doesn't kill me," she said to herself, "before he takes a second look at me, he'll say I look like a Coney Island chorus girl. But what could I do—oh! what could I do with a dollar and eighty-seven cents?"

NARRATOR. At 7 o'clock the coffee was made and the frying-pan was on the back of the stove hot and ready to cook the chops. Jim was never late.

DELLA. Della doubled the fob chain in her hand and sat on the corner of the table near the door that he always entered. Then she heard his step on the stair away down on the first flight, and she turned white for just a moment.

NARRATOR. She had a habit of saying little silent prayers about the simplest everyday things, and now she whispered:

DELLA. "Please God, make him think I am still pretty."

NARRATOR. The door opened and Jim stepped in and closed it. He looked thin and very serious. Poor fellow, he was only twenty-two—and to be burdened with a family! He needed a new overcoat and he was without gloves.

JIM. Jim stopped inside the door, as immovable as a setter at the scent of quail. His eyes were fixed upon Della, and there was an expression in them that she could not read, and it terrified her. It was not anger, nor surprise, nor disapproval, nor horror, nor any of the sentiments that she had been prepared for. He simply stared at her fixedly with that peculiar expression on his face.

DELLA. Della wriggled off the table and went for him. "Jim, darling," she cried, "don't look at me that way. I had my hair cut off and sold it because I couldn't have lived through Christmas without giving you a present. It'll grow out again—you won't mind, will you? I just had to do it. My hair grows awfully fast. Say 'Merry Christmas!' Jim, and let's be happy. You don't know what a nice—what a beautiful, nice gift I've got for you."

JIM. (Laboriously.) "You've cut off your hair?"

DELLA. "Cut it off and sold it! Don't you like me just as well, anyhow? I'm me without my hair, ain't I?"

JIM. (Looking about curiously.) "You say your hair is gone?"

DELLA. "You needn't look for it. It's sold, I tell you—sold and gone, too. It's Christmas Eve, boy. Be good to me, for it went for you. Maybe the hairs of my head were numbered, but nobody could ever count my love for you. Shall I put the chops on, Jim?"

NARRATOR. Out of his trance Jim seemed quickly to wake. He enfolded his Della. For ten seconds let us regard with discreet scrutiny some inconsequential object in the other direction. Eight dollars a week or a million a year—what is the difference? A mathematician or a wit would give you the wrong answer. The magi brought valuable gifts, but that was not among them. This dark assertion will be illuminated later on.

Jim drew a package from his overcoat pocket and threw it upon the table.

JIM. "Don't make any mistake, Dell, about me. I don't think there's anything in the way of a haircut or a shave or a shampoo that could make me like my girl any less. But if you'll unwrap that package you may see why you had me going a while at first."

NARRATOR. White fingers and nimble tore at the string and paper. And then an ecstatic scream of joy; and then, alas! a quick feminine change to hysterical tears and wails, necessitating the immediate employment of all the comforting powers of the lord of the flat.

For there lay The Combs—the set of combs, side and back, that Della had worshipped for long in a Broadway window. Beautiful combs, pure tortoise shell, with jewelled rims—just the shade to wear in the beautiful vanished hair. They were expensive combs, she knew, and her heart had simply craved and yearned over them without the least hope of possession. And now, they were hers, but the tresses that should have adorned the coveted adornments were gone.

DELLA. But she hugged them to her bosom, and at length she was able to look up with dim eyes and a smile and say: "My hair grows so fast, Jim!" And then she cried, "Oh!"

NARRATOR. Jim had not yet seen his beautiful present. She held it out to him eagerly upon her open palm. The dull precious metal seemed to flash with a reflection of her bright and ardent spirit.

DELLA. "Isn't it a dandy, Jim? I hunted all over town to find it. You'll have to look at the time a hundred times a day now. Give me your watch. I want to see how it looks on it."

NARRATOR. Instead of obeying, Jim tumbled down on the couch and put his hands under the back of his head and smiled.

JIM. "Dell, let's put our Christmas presents away and keep 'em a while. They're too nice to use just at present. I sold the watch to get the money to buy your combs. And now suppose you put the chops on."

NARRATOR. The magi, as you know, were wise men—wonderfully wise men—who brought gifts to the Babe in the manger. They invented the art of giving Christmas presents. Being wise, their gifts were no doubt wise ones, possibly bearing the privilege of exchange in case of duplication. And here we have lamely related to you the uneventful chronicle of two foolish children in a flat who most unwisely sacrificed for each other the greatest treasures of their house. But in a last word to the wise of these days let it be said that of all who give gifts these two were the wisest.

DELLA. Of all who give and receive gifts, such as they are wisest.

DELLA *and* **JIM.** Everywhere they are wisest.

NARRATOR. They are the magi.

Jean Valjean and the Bishop's Candlesticks

from Les Misérables by Victor Hugo

This beautiful classic still has a lot of mileage in it, with its touching story of the power of love to reclaim human personality. I have edited the story to reduce repetition and update some of the language, but its strength and beauty survive the adapter's scissors. Characterization is important: the BISHOP must sound very kind but not naïve; JEAN is gruff but not stupid; MADAME MAGLOIRE is anxious and uncomprehending; the GENDARME is courteous and confused; the NARRATOR is the storyteller and must command the audience's attention and paint the scene with vivid colors in their minds.

NARRATOR. The door of the Bishop's house opened. A man entered. He had his knapsack on his back, his stick in his hand, and a rough, hard, tired, and fierce look in his eyes, as seen by the firelight. He was hideous.

Madame Magloire didn't even have the strength to scream. Mademoiselle Baptistine turned, saw the man enter, and started up half alarmed; then, slowly turning back again toward the fire, she looked at her brother, and her face resumed its usual calm and serene look.

The Bishop looked at the man quietly. As he was opening his mouth to speak to the invader of his home, the stranger spoke first.

JEAN. *(Harshly.)* See here! My name is Jean Valjean. I am a convict; I have been in the galleys nineteen years. Four days ago I was set free, and started for Pontarlier, which is my destination; during those four days I have walked from Toulon. Today I have walked twelve leagues. This evening, when I reached this place, I went to an inn, and they sent me away on account of my yellow passport, which I had shown at the mayor's office, as was necessary. I went to another inn; they said, "Get out!" It was the same with one as with another; nobody would have me. There in the square I lay down upon a stone; a good woman showed me your house and said, "Knock there!" I have knocked. What is this place, an inn? I have money. I am very tired—twelve leagues on foot! And I am hungry. Can I stay?

BISHOP. *(Calmly.)* Madame Magloire, put on another plate.

JEAN. *(Surprised.)* Wait! I am a galley slave, a convict, don't you see? Look . . . *(Holding up imaginary document.)* Here is what they have put in the passport: "Jean Valjean, a liberated convict, has been nineteen years in the galleys: five years for burglary, fourteen years for having attempted four times to escape. This man is very dangerous." There you have it! Is this an inn? Can you give me something to eat and a place to sleep? Have you got a stable?

BISHOP. Madame Magloire, put some sheets on the bed in the alcove. *(She exits.)* Monsieur, sit down and warm yourself. We are going to have our supper, and your bed will be prepared for you while you eat.

JEAN. *(Incredulous.)* What? You will keep me? You won't drive me away? *(Musing, half to himself.)* You call me *Monsieur* and don't say, "Get out, dog!" as the others do. Ahhh! It is nineteen years since I slept on a bed. *(Almost apologetically.)* I beg your pardon, Monsieur Innkeeper, what is your name? I will pay. You are a fine man. You are an innkeeper, aren't you?

BISHOP. I am a priest who lives here.

JEAN. You are the curé, aren't you? The pastor of this parish? Yes, of course. How stupid I am. I didn't notice your cap.

NARRATOR. While speaking, Jean had deposited his knapsack and stick in the corner, returned his passport to his pocket, and sat down.

JEAN. You are humane, Monsieur curé; you don't despise me. A good priest is a good thing . . . Then you don't want me to pay you?

BISHOP. No. Keep your money.

NARRATOR. Madame Magloire brought in a plate and set it on the table. Then the Bishop asked her for more light, and she brought the two silver candlesticks from his bedchamber—lovely pieces—and lighted the candles, and placed them on the table.

JEAN. *(Noticing the candlesticks.)* Monsieur curé, you are good; you don't despise me. You take me into your house, and you light your candles for me, and I haven't hid from you where I come from, and how desperate I am. And you have not asked my name.

BISHOP. You need not tell me who you are. This is not my house; it is the house of Christ. It does not ask any comer whether he has a name, but whether he has an affliction. You are suffering; you are hungry and thirsty; be welcome. And do not thank me. Do not tell me that I take you into *my* house. This is the home of no man, except him who needs sanctuary. I tell you, a traveler, that you are more at home here than I—whatever is here is yours. What need have I to know your name? Besides . . . before you told me, I knew it.

JEAN. *(Suspicious now.)* Really? You knew my name?

BISHOP. Yes. Your name is my brother. *(Jean sighs with muffled relief.)* You have seen much suffering?

JEAN. *(Thinking hard.)* Ahhh . . . The red shirt, the ball and chain, the plank to sleep on . . . the heat, the cold, the galley's crew, the lash, the double chain for nothing, the dungeon for a word! Even when sick in bed—the chain! The dogs . . . The dogs are happier.

BISHOP. You have certainly left a place of suffering. But listen: there will be more joy in heaven over the tears of a repentant sinner than over the white robes of a hundred good men.

NARRATOR. Meanwhile Madame Magloire had served the supper: soup, pork, mutton, oil, bread, and salt; a few figs, a green cheese, and a large loaf of rye bread. The Bishop said the blessing, and then served the soup himself, as was his custom. The man attacked the food greedily, but the Bishop paused.

BISHOP. It seems to me that something is lacking on the table.

NARRATOR. Madame Magloire had set out just the three plates that were necessary. But it was the custom of the house, when the Bishop had anyone to supper, to set all six of the silver plates on the table. This graceful appearance of luxury was a kind of childlikeness that had a certain charm in this gentle but austere household, which elevated poverty to dignity.

Madame Magloire understood the Bishop's remark. Without a word she went out, and a moment later the three additional plates for which the Bishop had asked were shining on the cloth, symmetrically arranged before them.

Jean Valjean seemed to pay little attention to this, but continued eating hungrily like a starving man. After supper he and the Bishop had a brief conversation. Then, having told his sister good-night, the Bishop took one of the silver candlesticks from the table, handed the other to his guest, and said to him,

BISHOP. Monsieur, I will show you to your room.

NARRATOR. The house was arranged so that one could reach the alcove in the chapel only by passing through the Bishop's bedroom. They were passing through this room just as Madame Magloire was putting away the silver in the cupboard at the head of the bed, the last thing she did each night at bedtime. The Bishop left his guest in the alcove, before a clean white bed, and the stranger put the candlestick upon a small table.

BISHOP. Now, a good night's rest to you! Tomorrow morning, before you go, you shall have a cup of warm milk from our cows.

JEAN. *(Abruptly, with a menacing gesture.)* Hah! Indeed! You let me sleep in your house, as near to you as that! *(With a horrible laugh.)* Have you reflected upon it? Who tells you that I am not a murderer?

BISHOP. *(After a moment.)* God will take care of that.

(A brief interval.)

NARRATOR. The next day, at sunrise, Monseigneur the Bishop was walking in his garden. Madame Magloire ran toward him, quite upset.

MAGLOIRE. Monseigneur, Monseigneur! Do you know where the silver basket is?

BISHOP. *(Suspiciously calm.)* Yes.

NARRATOR. The Bishop had just found the basket in a flower bed.

BISHOP. There it is.

MAGLOIRE. But—there is nothing in it. The silver!

BISHOP. Ah. It is the silver then that troubles you. I do not know where that is.

MAGLOIRE. Good heavens! It is stolen. That man who came last night and left already this morning took it! The silver is stolen!

BISHOP. *(Thoughtfully.)* Hmmm. First, did this silver belong to us? Madame Magloire, I have for a long time wrongfully withheld this silver. It belonged to the poor. Who was this man? A poor man, evidently.

MAGLOIRE. Oh, my! My goodness! It is not on my account or mademoiselle's that I am disturbed—it is all the same to us. But what about you, Monseigneur? What is monsieur going to eat from now?

BISHOP. Have we no tin plates?

MAGLOIRE. Tin smells.

BISHOP. Well, then, iron plates.

MAGLOIRE. Iron tastes.

BISHOP. Well, then, wooden plates.

NARRATOR. Soon the Bishop was eating breakfast at the same table at which he had eaten with Jean the night before. While eating, Monseigneur the Bishop pleasantly remarked to his sister, who said nothing, and to Madame Magloire, who was grumbling to herself, that there was really not even need for a wooden spoon or fork to dip a piece of bread into a cup of milk. . . . Then, as they were rising from the table . . . *(Knocking.)*

BISHOP. Come in!

NARRATOR. The door opened. A strange, fierce group appeared on the threshold. Three men were holding a fourth by the collar. The three men were gendarmes; the fourth, Jean Valjean. An officer, who appeared to lead the group, advanced toward the Bishop.

GENDARME. Monseigneur!

JEAN. *(Astonished.)* Monseigneur! Then it is not the curé!

GENDARME. Silence! It is Monseigneur, the Bishop. *(An awkward pause.)*

BISHOP. Ah . . . so it is you, Jean. I am glad to see you. But . . . I would have given you the candlesticks also, which are silver like the rest and would bring you two hundred francs. Why did you not take them along with your plates?

NARRATOR. Jean Valjean looked at the Bishop with an indescribable expression on his face.

GENDARME. Monseigneur, then what this man said was true? When we met him he was going like a man who was running away, and we arrested him to check on it. He had this silver.

BISHOP. And he told you that it had been given him by an old priest with whom he had passed the night. I see it all. And you brought him back here? It is all a mistake.

GENDARME. Well, if that is so . . . we can let him go.

BISHOP. Certainly.

JEAN. *(Stupified; looking from one to the other.)* Is it true that they let me go?

GENDARME. Yes, yes. Don't you understand?

BISHOP. My friend, before you leave, here are your candlesticks. Take them.

NARRATOR. Jean Valjean was trembling violently. He took the two candlesticks mechanically, with a wild look in his eyes.

BISHOP. Now go in peace. By the way, my friend, when you come again, you need not come through the garden. You can always come in and go out by the front door. It is closed only with a latch, day or night.

NARRATOR. After the gendarmes left the house, the Bishop approached Jean Valjean, who felt like a man about to faint.

BISHOP. *(In a low, intense voice.)* Forget not—never forget—that you have promised me to use this silver to become an honest man.

NARRATOR. Jean Valjean, who did not remember making such a promise, stood stunned.

BISHOP. Jean Valjean, my brother, you belong no longer to evil, but to good. It is your soul that I am buying for you. I withdraw it from dark thought and from the spirit of perdition, and I give it to God.

The reading might conclude here, but if you wish to include the following episode it would show the effect of Jean's encounter with the Bishop on the convict's life. In addition to the NARRATOR and JEAN, two more characters are required—the BOY and the PRIEST. They could be read by the person who reads the GENDARME.

NARRATOR. Jean Valjean escaped hurriedly from the city into the open country, taking the first lanes and paths he found, without noticing that at times he was retracing his steps. He wandered about all morning. He had eaten nothing, but he felt no hunger. He felt somewhat angry but knew not against whom. He could not tell whether he had been helped or humiliated. Unspeakable thoughts gathered in his mind the whole day.

Late afternoon, as the sun was sinking toward the horizon, Jean Valjean was seated behind a thicket in a large reddish plain, an absolute desert. There was no horizon but the Alps.

While he was thinking, he heard a little Savoyard, about twelve years old, coming along the path singing, with a barrel organ at his side and a marmot box on his back—one of those pleasant youngsters who wander from place to place, with their knees sticking through their trousers. Always singing, the boy stopped occasionally, and playfully tossed up some coins, probably his whole fortune. Among them was one forty-sous piece.

The boy stopped beside the thicket without seeing Jean Valjean, and threw his handful of sous into the air. He skillfully caught them all on the back of his hand—except the forty-sous piece, which rolled toward the thicket, near Jean Valjean. . . . Jean Valjean put his foot on it. The boy, however, had seen where it went.

BOY. *(Brightly, unafraid.)* Monsieur—my coin?

JEAN. What is your name?

BOY. Petit Gervais, Monsieur.

JEAN. *(Gruffly.)* Get out.

BOY. Monsieur, give me my coin. *(Jean Valjean drops his head, not hearing.)* My money! My silver piece!

NARRATOR. Jean Valjean did not appear to understand. The boy took him
by the collar of his shirt and shook him. At the same time he tried to
move the big iron-soled shoe which was covering the treasure.

BOY. I want my money! My forty-sous piece!

NARRATOR. The child began to cry. Jean Valjean raised his head. His look
was disturbed as he absently reached for his stick.

JEAN. *(Coming out of his daze slowly.)* Who is there?

BOY. Me, Monsieur! Petit Gervais! Me! Give me my forty sous, please! Why
don't you move your foot?

JEAN. Ahhh! You here yet! *(With cold malice.)* You'd better watch out for
yourself!

NARRATOR. The boy looked at him in terror—then fled without daring to
turn his head or even scream. In a moment or two he was gone.

　　　The sun had gone down. Jean Valjean shivered. He was aware
of the cold night air. He pulled his cap down over his forehead,
mechanically tried to button his shirt, and then stooped to pick up his
stick. At that moment he saw the forty-sous piece which his foot had
half buried in the ground. It came as an electric shock.

JEAN. What—is—that?

NARRATOR. Convulsively he seized the piece of money and stood up,
looking away over the plain, straining his eyes toward all points of the
horizon, trembling like a frightened deer seeking a place of refuge.

JEAN. *(With sudden realization.)* Oh!

NARRATOR. He began to walk rapidly in the direction in which the child
had gone.

JEAN. *(Calling.)* Petit Gervais! Petit Gervais!

NARRATOR. There was no answer. The country was desolate and gloomy.
On all sides was space. There was nothing about him but a shadow in
which his gaze was lost, and a silence in which his voice was lost.

JEAN. Petit Gervais! Petit Gervais!

NARRATOR. Doubtless the boy was already far away. But soon a priest
came riding up on horseback. Jean Valjean frantically waved him to
a stop.

JEAN. Monsieur curé, have you seen a child go by?

PRIEST. No.

JEAN. Petit Gervais was his name.

PRIEST. I have seen nobody.

NARRATOR. Jean took two five-franc pieces from his bag and gave them
to the priest.

JEAN. This is for your poor. Monsieur curé, he is a little fellow, about ten years old, with a marmot, I think, and a barrel organ. He went this way. One of these Savoyards, you know.

PRIEST. I have not see him.

JEAN. Is his village near here? Can you tell me?

PRIEST. If it be as you say, my friend, the little fellow is a foreigner. They roam abut this country. Nobody knows them.

NARRATOR. Valjean hastily took out two more five-franc pieces and gave them to the priest.

JEAN. For your poor. *(Wildly.)* Monsieur abbé, have me arrested! I am a robber!

NARRATOR. The priest put spurs to his horse, and fled in great fear. Jean Valjean, exhausted, despising himself, sank to his knees and burst into tears. It was the first time he had wept for nineteen years.

As he wept, he beheld himself, so to speak, face to face; at the same time he saw, at a mysterious distance, a sort of light which he thought at first was a torch. Examining more attentively this light which had dawned upon his conscience, he recognized that it had a human form, and that this torch was the Bishop.

And as he wept, the light grew brighter in his mind—a light extraordinary, at once transporting and terrible. His past life, his first offense, his long expiation, his brutal exterior, his hardened interior, his release made glad by so many schemes of vengeance, what had happened to him at the Bishop's, his last action, this theft of forty sous from a child, a crime meaner and the more monstrous in that it came after the Bishop's pardon—all this returned and appeared to him, clearly, but in a light he had never seen before. He beheld his life, and it seemed to him horrible; his soul, and it seemed to him frightful. There was, however, a softened light upon that life and upon that soul. It seemed to him that he was looking upon Satan by the light of Paradise.

How long did he cry? What did he do afterward? Where did he go? Nobody ever knew. It is known simply that on that very night, the stage-driver who drove at that time on the Grenoble route and arrived at the town about three o'clock in the morning, saw, as he passed through the Bishop's street, a man in the attitude of prayer kneel upon the pavement in the shadow, before the door of the Monseigneur.

The Great Divorce
from the fantasy by C. S. Lewis

Writings of the late C. S. Lewis are a potential gold mine for those interested in Christian Readers Theatre. His space-fiction trilogy, his delightful
Screwtape Letters, and certainly *The Great Divorce* are full of spiritual
insights delivered through imaginative settings, lively dialogue, and very
human character portrayals. A number of scenes from *The Great Divorce*
would illustrate worship themes. The following selection, for three readers
—the NARRATOR, a SPIRIT, and a GHOST—begins with narrative background supplied by the adapter.

Reprinted with permission of The Macmillan Company from *The Great Divorce* by C. S. Lewis. Copyright 1946 by The Macmillan Company. For performance rights, apply to: Geoffrey Bles, Ltd., c/o William Collins Sons & Co.,
Ltd., 14 St. James's Place, London, S.W. 1, England.

NARRATOR. *The Great Divorce* is a fantasy written by C. S. Lewis. The
divorce he refers to is the divorce between heaven and hell, and he
is saying that there is a great gulf fixed between them. He seems to
be saying that if we insist on holding on to Hell—which generally
turns out to be the human ego—we shall never see Heaven.

The story begins in Grey Town, which is the name given to the
place where the dead exist, those who have not gone directly to the
High Country, or Heaven. Grey Town is a dim, murky place where
nobody seems very happy or very sad and where the sun never quite
sets and never quite rises.

Occasionally some people from Grey Town take a bus trip to
the plains where they can view, off in the distance, the High Country.
With the author himself, we board such a bus and take the trip toward
the High Country. On disembarking, we are disturbed by the hard-
ness of everything—even the grass under our feet is painfully hard—
for such is the solidity of reality! As we look about we see the high

mountains in the distance. Soon there appear Bright Spirits coming from the mountains to talk to us who have come from Grey Town. They are friends or relatives of the people—or rather, Ghosts—from Grey Town. The Spirits try to persuade the Ghosts to return with them to the High Country where truth may be found and God known. But the Ghosts, for various reasons, are unwilling to make the long, difficult journey up into the mountains. Here is one of the Bright Spirits approaching a rather startled Ghost:

SPIRIT. *(Loudly.)* Don't you know me?

GHOST. Well, I'm damned. I wouldn't have believed it. . . . *(Quite upset.)* It isn't right, Len, you know. What about poor Jack, eh? You look pretty pleased with yourself, but what I say is, What about poor Jack?

SPIRIT. He is here. You will meet him soon, if you stay.

GHOST. But you murdered him.

SPIRIT. Of course I did. It is all right now.

GHOST. All right, is it? All right for you, you mean. But what about the poor chap himself, lying cold and dead?

SPIRIT. But he isn't. I have told you, you will meet him soon. He sent you his love.

GHOST. What I'd like to understand is what you're here for, as pleased as Punch, you, a bloody murderer, while I've been walking the streets down there and living in a place like a pigstye all these years.

SPIRIT. That is a little hard to understand at first. But it is all over now. You will be pleased about it presently. Till then there is no need to bother about it.

GHOST. No need to bother about it? Aren't you ashamed of yourself?

SPIRIT. No. Not as you mean. I do not look at myself. I have given up myself. I had to, you know, after the murder. That was what it did for me. And that was how everything began.

GHOST. Personally, I'd have thought you and I ought to be the other way round. That's my personal opinion.

SPIRIT. Very likely we soon shall be. If you'll stop thinking about it.

GHOST. *(Slapping its chest.)* Look at me, now. I gone straight all my life. I don't say I was a religious man and I don't say I had no faults, far from it. But I done my best all my life, see? I done my best by everyone, that's the sort of chap I was. I never asked for anything that wasn't mine by rights. If I wanted a drink I paid for it and if I took my wages I done my job, see? That's the sort I was and I don't care who knows it.

SPIRIT. It would be much better not to go on about that now.

GHOST. Who's going on? I'm not arguing. I'm just telling you the sort of chap I was, see? I'm asking for nothing but my rights. You may think you can put me down because you're dressed up like that (which you weren't when you worked under me) and I'm only a poor man. But I got to have my rights same as you, see?

SPIRIT. Oh no. It's not so bad as that. I haven't got my rights, or I should not be here. You will not get yours either. You'll get something far better. Never fear.

GHOST. That's just what I say. I haven't got my rights. I always done my best and I never done nothing wrong. And what I don't see is why I should be put below a bloody murderer like you.

SPIRIT. Who knows whether you will be? Only be happy and come with me.

GHOST. What do you keep on arguing for? I'm only telling you the sort of chap I am. I only want my rights. I'm not asking for anybody's bleeding charity.

SPIRIT. Then do. At once. Ask for the Bleeding Charity. Everything is here for the asking and nothing can be bought.

GHOST. That may be very well for you, I daresay. If they choose to let in a bloody murderer all because he makes a poor mouth at the last moment, that's their look out. But I don't see myself going in the same boat with you, see? Why should I? I don't want charity. I'm a decent man and if I had my rights I'd have been here long ago and you can tell them I said so.

SPIRIT. *(Shaking his head.)* You can never do it like that. Your feet will never grow hard enough to walk on our grass that way. You'd be tired out before we got to the mountains. And it isn't exactly true, you know.

GHOST. *(Sulkily.)* What isn't true?

SPIRIT. You weren't a decent man and you didn't do your best. We none of us were and we none of us did. Lord bless you, it doesn't matter. There is no need to go into it all now.

GHOST. You! *(Gasping.)* *You* have the face to tell *me* I wasn't a decent chap?

SPIRIT. Of course. Must I go into all that? I will tell you one thing to begin with. Murdering old Jack wasn't the worst thing I did. That was the work of a moment and I was half mad when I did it. But I murdered you in my heart, deliberately, for years. I used to lie awake at nights thinking what I'd do to you if ever I got the chance. That is why I have been sent to you now: to ask your forgiveness and to be your servant as long as you need one, and longer if it pleases you. I was the worst. But all the men who worked under you felt the same. You made it hard for us, you know. And you made it hard for your wife too and for your children.

GHOST. You mind your own business, young man. None of your lip, see? Because I'm not taking any impudence from you about my private affairs.

SPIRIT. There are no private affairs.

GHOST. And I'll tell you another thing. You can clear off, see? You're not wanted. I may be only a poor man but I'm not making pals with a murderer, let alone taking lessons from him. Made it hard for you and your like, did I? If I had you back there I'd show you what work is.

SPIRIT. *(With laughter in his voice.)* Come and show me now. It will be joy going to the mountains, but there will be plenty of work.

GHOST. You don't suppose I'd go with you?

SPIRIT. Don't refuse. You will never get there alone. And I am the one who was sent to you.

GHOST. So that's the trick, is it? *(Bitter but somehow triumphant.)* I thought there'd be some damned nonsense. It's all a clique, all a bloody clique. Tell them I'm not coming, see? I'd rather be damned than go along with you. I came here to get my rights, see? Not to go snivelling along on charity tied onto your apron-strings. If they're too fine to have me without you, I'll go home. That's what I'll do, I'll go home. I didn't come here to be treated like a dog. I'll go home. That's what I'll do. Damn and blast the whole pack of you . . .

NARRATOR. And the poor Ghost, grumbling and whimpering a little as it picked its way over the sharp grasses, made off. The Bright Spirit, we may assume, was disappointed at having to return to the High Country by himself.

An Enemy of the People
from Act II of the play by Henrik Ibsen

Here's a scene from one of Ibsen's masterful realistic dramas, edited to highlight the clash between the two brothers and abridged for inclusion in a worship service. Our performance involved four readers standing as a quartet on the chancel steps and using offstage focus. The play has an obvious relevance to our current ecological crisis; also it deals with questions of conscience and human integrity. In presenting the piece, we used a brief introduction by the NARRATOR to provide background. Besides the NARRATOR, the characters are PETER, THOMAS, KATRINA (his wife), and PETRA (their grown daughter), who may be read by the NARRATOR if desired.

NARRATOR. A small Norwegian village is the setting for Ibsen's drama *An Enemy of the People*. Dr. Thomas Stockmann, health officer of the village, has discovered impurities in the mineral baths from which the town is gaining its wealth. Dr. Stockmann finds himself fighting his own brother, Peter, the town's mayor, who wants to protect the town's financial interests. The brothers clash directly as the mayor irately invades the doctor's home . . .

PETER. Doctor, yesterday evening, after office hours, I received from you a dissertation upon the state of the water at the Baths.

THOMAS. Yes, Peter. Have you read it?

PETER. I have. (*A strained pause.*) As usual, you employ violent expressions in your statement. Among other things, you say that what we offer our visitors is a slow poison.

THOMAS. Why, Peter, what else can it be called? Just think—poisoned water taken both internally and externally! And we offer this to poor invalids who come to us in all confidence and pay us handsomely to cure them!

PETER. Have you taken the trouble to think what your proposed alterations would cost? From what the engineer said, I gathered that the expenses would probably amount to several hundred thousand crowns.

THOMAS. So much as that?

PETER. Yes. But that is not the worst. The work would take at least two years.

THOMAS. Two years! Do you mean to say two whole years?

PETER. At least. And what are we to do with the Baths in the meantime? Close them? We should have no alternative. And do you think that anyone would come here if it got abroad that the water was poisoned?

THOMAS. But, Peter, that's precisely what it is.

PETER. And all this now, just now, when the Baths are doing so well! There are some neighboring towns that claim also to be health resorts. Don't you think they would immediately set to work to divert the full stream of visitors to themselves? Undoubtedly they would; and we should be left stranded. We should probably have to abandon the whole costly undertaking; and then you would have ruined your native town.

THOMAS. I—ruined—!

PETER. I have not convinced myself that the condition of the water at the Baths is as serious as your statement represents.

THOMAS. I tell you, if anything it's worse—or will be in the summer, when the hot weather sets in. I tell you that, Peter; and it's my deepest, sincerest conviction—

PETER. As a health officer under the Board of Directors, you have no right to hold any individual conviction.

THOMAS. (Startled.) No right to—?

PETER. As an official, I say. In your private capacity, of course, it is another matter. But as a subordinate official of the Baths, you have no right to express any conviction that differs with that of your superiors.

THOMAS. This is too much! I, a doctor, a man of science, have no right to—!

PETER. The matter in question is not a purely scientific one; it is a complex affair; it has both a technical and an economic side.

THOMAS. What the devil do I care! I will be free to speak my mind on any subject under the sun!

PETER. As you please—so long as it does not concern the Baths. That we forbid.

THOMAS. (Shouts.) You forbid! You! A pack of—

PETER. I forbid it—I, your chief; and when I issue an order, you simply must obey.

THOMAS. Peter, if you weren't my brother—

PETRA. *(Entering.)* Father, you mustn't submit to this!

KATRINA. *(Entering.)* Petra, Petra!

THOMAS. The source is poisoned, man! Are you mad? We make our living by trafficking in filth and corruption! The whole of our flourishing social life is rooted in a lie!

PETER. Idle fancies—or worse. The man who scatters such offensive insinuations against his native place must be an enemy of society.

THOMAS. *(With a violent gesture.)* You dare to—!

KATRINA. Thomas!

PETRA. Keep calm, father!

PETER. *(Drawing up his dignity.)* I will not expose myself to violence. You have had your warning. Reflect upon what you owe to yourself and to your family. Good-bye. *(Exits from scene.)*

THOMAS. And I must put up with such treatment! In my own house, Katrina! What do you say to that!

KATRINA. Indeed, it's a shame and a disgrace, Thomas— But after all, your brother has the power—

THOMAS. Yes, but I have the right.

KATRINA. Oh yes, right, right! What good does it do to have the right, if you haven't any might?

PETRA. Oh, mother—how can you say that?

THOMAS. Do you mean it's no good, in a free community, to have right on your side? What an absurd idea, Katrina!

KATRINA. Why, good heavens, Thomas, you're surely not thinking of—?

THOMAS. What am I not thinking of?

KATRINA. —of setting yourself up against your own brother!

THOMAS. What the devil would you have me do, if not stick to what is right and truth? Ho-ho, Katrina! Just wait a while, and you shall see whether I can fight my battles to the end.

KATRINA. Yes, to the end of getting your dismissal; that's what will happen.

THOMAS. Well then, I shall at any rate have done my duty toward the public, toward society—I who am called an enemy of society!

KATRINA. But toward your family, Thomas? Toward us at home? Do you think that is doing your duty to those who are dependent on you?

PETRA. Oh, mother, don't always think first of us.

KATRINA. Yes, it's easy for you to talk; you can stand alone if necessary. But remember the boys, Thomas; and think a little of yourself too, and of me—

THOMAS. You're out of your senses, Katrina! If I were to be such a pitiful coward as to knuckle under to Peter and his confounded crew— should I ever have another happy hour in all my life?

KATRINA. I don't know about that; but God preserve us from the happiness we shall all of us have if you persist in defying them! There you will be again, with nothing to live on, with no regular income. I should think we had had enough of that in the old days. Remember them, Thomas; think of what it all means.

THOMAS. (Struggling with himself; clenching his hands, perhaps.) And this is what these jacks-in-office can bring upon a free and honest man! Isn't it revolting, Katrina?

KATRINA. Yes, no doubt they are treating you shamefully. But God knows there's plenty of injustice one must submit to in this world. Here are the boys, Thomas. Look at them! What is to become of them?

THOMAS. The boys—! (Pausing to reflect; then, recovering.) No, even if the whole earth should crumble, I will never bow my neck to this yoke!

KATRINA. Thomas—what are you going to do?

THOMAS. I must have the right to look my boys in the face when they have grown into free men. (Exits from scene.)

KATRINA. (Crying.) Ah, God help us all!

PETRA. Father is true to the core. He will never give in!

Lying Offshore

from the story by G. William Jones

This one, for a quartet of readers (two men and two women), seems to speak to the themes of evangelism, the nature of the church, and the mission of the church in the world. It could be a discussion starter in an informal setting or the springboard for launching the sermon on Sunday morning. The readers, each of whom is both narrator and character, would probably use offstage focus. It's a rather intense story and must be read that way.

WOMAN 1. A ship rocked slowly upon the greasy seas. Its sails were tattered, its masts spliced, and its hull leaky with worm-eaten planks, but still it stayed afloat. It had been sailing for many years—for generations actually.

MAN 1. Many years ago it had been loaded with food and medicine, and dispatched to find and to help the people of a lost colony. As it traveled far and wide, all its original crew except one had died, their places being taken by their children.

WOMAN 2. In the prow an old man, the last of the original crew, sat upon a coil of rope, his watery eyes struggling to pierce the fog. Below decks men, women, and children sat down to eat. Although the fare was meagre, it was adequate, and all their faces shone with health.

MAN 2. The meal was almost over when both doors of the messroom were thrown open with a loud noise and a rush of wind. In the opening stood an old man, strange and wild, stronger than they had ever seen him!

MAN 1. *(Shouting.)* We're here! We've arrived at land!

WOMAN 1. Land?

WOMAN 2. Did you say—land?

W 1 *and* M 2. What land?

MAN 1. Why . . . the land we were sent to when this voyage began. And the lost colony is there waiting! I can hear them shouting from the shore! Quick! Let's make for shore and unload the food and the medicine!

WOMAN 1. The old man turned to run back up the gangway, but stopped halfway up when he realized there had been no movement in the messroom. Slowly he returned to stare at them with wide, incredulous eyes, his mouth agape.

MAN 1. Didn't you hear me? I said we're here! The people we were sent out to help are only a few hundred yards away. But we must hurry, for they are all hungry and sick!

MAN 2. *(Shrugs.)* I'm sure we'd all like to help those people. But—as you can see—there's hardly enough food and medicine here to take care of us and our children.

WOMAN 2. Besides, we don't know what kind of people they are. Who knows *what* might happen if we landed and went among them?

WOMAN 1. The old man staggered back as if he had been struck in the face.

MAN 1. But . . . but . . . it was for *them* that this voyage began in the first place so many years ago, for *them* that the ship was built, for *them* that the food and medicine were stowed aboard!

MAN 2. Yes, old man, I've heard *many* tales of our launching from my father and from the other old men who are now dead, but there were so many different accounts that how can we be sure which one is right? Why risk our stores and provisions, perhaps even our lives, on something we may not even be supposed to do?

WOMAN 2. That's right!

WOMAN 1. Sure. It's a terrible risk!

MAN 1. But look, it's all very simple! As far as there not being enough food for us *and* them, much of what we have left is meant for *seed*! If we go ashore and *plant* it, then there will be more than enough for all. And on the matter of *why* the ship was launched in the first place— you have merely to look in the logbook. It's all there.

WOMAN 1. The old man, hoping he had settled the question, looked anxiously from face to face around the table. There was a long, thoughtful silence. . . . Finally, a man who had gravitated to a position of leadership among them stood up, picking his teeth and frowning thoughtfully.

MAN 2. Perhaps the old man is right. At any rate, his suggestion merits investigation. What I propose is this: let us select from among ourselves a representative committee which will see if they can find the old logbook, and then go into a thorough study of it, to see if they can determine whether we should land or not.

WOMAN 1. Right!

WOMAN 2. That's a sensible idea!

WOMAN 1. Let's do it!

MAN 1. What *is* this? What are you *doing*?

WOMAN 1. The old man, now frantic from hearing the cries from shore, backed away from them with horror in his eyes.

MAN 1. I can see that you do not really expect to do anything at all!

WOMAN 1. His back against a bulkhead, he clutched at his chest and slid weakly to the floor.

MAN 1. Let me warn you then. The food will not last. It was meant to stay preserved only for the time it would take to get here. Now the food will begin to molder, and the medicines will separate and lose their strength. If you do not take the provisions ashore and share them, they will soon no longer feed or cure even you!

WOMAN 1. And with this, he died.

MAN 2. As the days and weeks passed, the ship continued to lie offshore. The committee continued to search the logbook, which they had soon found, hoping to come up with a report "in the near future."

WOMAN 2. A few of the younger men and women, maddened with the waiting and lured irresistibly by the cries of hunger and pain from the shore, slipped away one night in the jolly boat with a few provisions and were listed sorrowfully next day as "lost at sea."

MAN 1. True to the old man's dying prophecy, the food on board began to grow all manner of weird and exotic fungi, and the extensive stores of medicine seemed less and less able to cure the ills of the people. Also, the cries from shore began to grow so loud that even the deafest on board had to stuff his ears with cotton in order to sleep.

WOMAN 1. But no one seemed to be able to decide what to do.

Where Have All the Flowers Gone?

from a newspaper column by Al Martinez
adapted for Readers Theatre by Melvin R. White

Here's a delightful but sobering piece on the pollution crisis for NARRA-
TOR, FATHER, and BOY (the NARRATOR could be male or female), which
makes some other points besides ecology, if I read the FATHER's last
speech right. At any rate, you'll have some fun with this one if you keep
it conversational and make the FATHER sound very nostalgic. Genesis
1:26–31 might be the parallel text if your theme is man's use of his world.

"Where Have All the Flowers Gone?" by Al Martinez, appeared in the *Oak-
land Tribune*, February 10, 1970. Used by permission.

NARRATOR. Once upon a time in the year 2000, a small boy walked up to
  his father and asked,
BOY. Daddy, where did I come from?
NARRATOR. The man looked around frantically for his wife, but she wasn't
  there and the child persisted, so it was up to the father.
FATHER. Sit down, son.
NARRATOR. The air purification unit was turned up high, and the green
  lights on the door panel showed that the house was hermetically
  sealed, so neither the man nor the boy wore his oxygen mask.
FATHER. Lad, I guess it's time I told you about the birds and the bees.
BOY. *(Frowning.)* The what and the what?
FATHER. *(Laughing.)* The birds and the bees. You've seen pictures of
  them. They lived ... *(remembering)* ... they lived in the days of clean
  air when such life was abundant on earth. Before oxygen masks and
  sealed homes. Before night was heavy blackness and day a dirty twi-
  light. In the days when little boys like you played outside.
BOY. *(Amazed.)* Out in that?

BISHOP. "I did. He won't take that for an answer. But it seems to me . . ."

ME. . . . the bishop went on, beating around the bush again . . .

BISHOP. ". . . that any approach to the problem must be experience-centered—one that the young student can incorporate into his being and reflect. . . ."

ME. *(Joyfully.)* "You're right! Experience! That's the ticket! Now supposing next Sunday you look down from the pulpit and find the devil sitting in the front pew. How's that for an experience?"

BISHOP. *(Upset.)* "In my church?"

ME. The bishop looked stunned.

BISHOP. "In the front pew?"

ME. "Oh, he'd be down front all right. Not crowded in the back with the rest of the congregation. They say he's a bold fellow, you know. Probably pleasant-looking, too. Shoes shined, good silk suit, handkerchief in pocket. But *you'd* know him, bishop. *You'd* sense the dark presence of evil, wouldn't you?"

BISHOP. "I would?"

ME. "And you'd denounce him for the terrible and ancient adversary that he is, wouldn't you? And you'd chase him down the aisle and kick him down the front steps, wouldn't you? Or cast him in the fiery furnace in the basement, wouldn't you? Or put him in the lockup for a thousand years?"

BISHOP. *(Severely.)* "A situation such as you describe cannot be acted upon without thorough and prolonged study. In fact, any attempt to drive anyone out of the church would undoubtedly be taken as a rebirth of intolerance."

ME. "I never thought of it exactly that way. Then what do you suggest?"

BISHOP. "Why, I should hope I'd be open-minded enough to invite him to a panel discussion with the Wednesday afternoon study group, or perhaps to the pulpit the following Sunday."

ME. "Marvelous! Then the congregation can jeer and mock him! Or even throw tomatoes at him!"

BISHOP. "Of course not!"

ME. The bishop looked pained as he led me down the garden path.

BISHOP. "There will be no emotionalism! After all, if the devil thinks he belongs in the church, then he should be accorded the right to expound his theories as best he may in an atmosphere of restraint and calm. There is no denying that the devil is an able theologian, and one can think him mistaken without hounding him like a heretic."

ME. I picked a raspberrry from a nearby shrub. "You mean any attempt to heave him out of the church would hurt the church's image more than the devil's?"

BISHOP. "Now you're beginning to get the idea."

ME. I gave him the raspberry. "But supposing the congregation decide they'd rather have the devil than you. That might do you out of a job."

BISHOP. *(Laughing.)* "Nonsense, my dear chap."

ME. And the bishop laughed so heartily I had to whack him on the back to bring him round. Then, wiping away tears of laughter, he walked toward his red sports car in the driveway.

BISHOP. "You are assuming that my congregation will see no difference between the devil's old heresies and my new and radical insights, which, as you know, are as fresh as the breezes in this garden."

ME. "I'm certainly glad they're not cold blasts from outer darkness." But the bishop couldn't hear me. He was off to the university with engine roaring and horn tootling like a loud but uncertain trumpet.

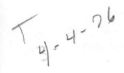

Prologue to Morning

from the poem by Hermann Hagedorn

Here's a stirring and profound free-verse poem (by the author of *The Bomb That Fell on America*) which required no adaptation, since it was written in dialogue. Questions of staging and interpretation arise. Perhaps EVERYMAN could stand center stage or on the chancel steps with the WATCHMAN speaking from the balcony, or at least in the rear of the auditorium. The WATCHMAN might read his lines with a strong, prolonged voice, as if speaking from a great distance. EVERYMAN might speak similarly at first, calling the WATCHMAN, but later becoming rather conversational. Or, you might want to put the WATCHMAN on your PA system, unseen by the congregation. Another variation would be to give the EVERYMAN lines to two voices (perhaps male and female) reading in unison, or individually for some lines and in unison for others. This poem could be a powerful sermon, call to worship, or benediction to a service. With its stress on the divine-human partnership and beginning anew, it provides a tremendous antidote to disappointment and despair.

"Prologue to Morning" is included here by permission of Mrs. Dorothea H. Parfit, 1207 North Western Avenue, Hollywood, Calif. 90029.

EVERYMAN. Watchman, what of the night?
WATCHMAN. The night has no stars and the winds are rising.
EVERYMAN. Watchman, what of the sea?
WATCHMAN. The sea is wild, and the shores are strewn with ships.
EVERYMAN. Watchman—
WATCHMAN. I hear.
EVERYMAN. What of the hearts of men?
WATCHMAN. They are as the night, and as the sea.
EVERYMAN. Watchman, I am Everyman, and I am troubled.
Where is my hope?
WATCHMAN. Your hope is where it *has* been.
EVERYMAN. Watchman, your answer is dark.

WATCHMAN.   To your mind, but not to your heart. Let the heart
              Listen and it will hear,
              Though the winds cry and the seas break.

EVERYMAN.   My heart is open.

WATCHMAN.   What does it hear?

EVERYMAN.   Storm.

WATCHMAN.   What else?

EVERYMAN.   A crying, as of a child lost in the dark.

WATCHMAN.   A crying?

EVERYMAN.   A fury, as of a child destroying his toys.

WATCHMAN.   No more?

EVERYMAN.   A Voice.

WATCHMAN.   A Voice?

EVERYMAN.   A Voice that cries, Think!

WATCHMAN.   What else?

EVERYMAN.   A Voice that calls, Aspire!

WATCHMAN.   What more?

EVERYMAN.   A Voice that whispers, Believe!

WATCHMAN.   Bow down, and hear!

EVERYMAN.   A Voice that commands, Dare!

WATCHMAN.   Lift up your eyes!

EVERYMAN.   Watchman, what have I heard?

WATCHMAN.   You have heard God speaking to Moses and to Socrates;
              To Jesus in the lonely places,
              To Isaiah and Amos and Micah,
              And Peter and John and Paul and Francis and Joan.
              You have heard God speaking to all His saints
              Who have fought for the recognition of His glory,
              And for liberation, and the expansion of the imprisoned,
                 the dwarfed spirit.
              You have heard God speaking to the men who dared the
                 seas to build a new nation,
              To Franklin and Washington and Jefferson
              And all the makers of the immortal Declaration
              That utters the hunger for life, for liberty, and the right of
                 man to be free of the chain, the bars, and the whip.
              You have heard God speaking to Abraham Lincoln—
              And to you.

EVERYMAN.   To me? What am I that the God Who spoke to these
              Should speak to me?

WATCHMAN.   What does the Voice say, the Voice in the heart?

EVERYMAN.   The Voice says, You are of the great succession.

Men have torn down, men have broken, men have destroyed.

It is yours to build, says the Voice, yours to build.

Out of the disaster of hate to bring the miracle of love.

Out of the fury of destruction to bring a new creation.

By men has the world been brought low.

By men shall the world again be lifted up.

By men and the Voice of God.

WATCHMAN.   The Voice of God is calling through the world!

EVERYMAN.   It is calling to me.

I hear!

WATCHMAN.   What does the Voice say, the Voice in the heart?

EVERYMAN.   The Voice says, Everyman,

I have a burden for you and a splendor.

You are the end of things—

Or a new world.

Think!

Believe!

Aspire!

Dare!

WATCHMAN.   What more?

EVERYMAN.   The Voice says, Day and night, let your heart listen.

WATCHMAN.   What is your answer, Everyman?

EVERYMAN.   My heart is listening. . . .

WATCHMAN.   Then the new world is born.

The Waiting Room

a play by Gordon C. Bennett

This is a one-act, running about thirty minutes. It attempts to raise searching questions about the world order, justice, poverty, faith, risk, and commitment, and is best used to promote discussion. Written for three men and three women (with the ANGEL probably female), the play requires no editing to make it Readers Theatre; the entire action takes place in one imaginary room, and the audience will catch on easily. In chapter four a suggested staging is given (see figure 6), and the directions given here assume that design, using offstage focus. The BUTCHER and the ANGEL are the key readers. Cast the former as gruff and overbearing, with perhaps an urban accent; the ANGEL must be a trifle scatterbrained.

At the beginning the readers doing WOMAN 1, WOMAN 2, MAN 1, *and* MAN 2 *are in the scene; the* BUTCHER *and the* ANGEL *are out. Overhead or on the back wall are two large signs reading "No Waiting" and "Immediate Delivery."*

WOMAN 1. *(After a suspenseful silence.)* This must be the worst part of it.

MAN 1. You mean—now?

WOMAN 1. Now. Waiting. Why do we have to wait so long?

MAN 1. It hasn't been long.

WOMAN 1. Well, it seems long to me. The signs say: No Waiting. Immediate Delivery.

MAN 2. It's just been a few minutes.

WOMAN 1. Really?

MAN 2. Really.

WOMAN 1. Are you sure?

MAN 1. We're sure, we're sure!

WOMAN 1. *(Unsatisfied.)* It seems long to me.

MAN 1. Don't worry about it. You can't make it come any sooner by thinking about it.

WOMAN 1. I know . . . but still. . . . Do you think it's going to hurt?

MAN 1. What?

WOMAN 1. Hurt.

MAN 1. *(Definitely.)* No.

WOMAN 1. Why not?

MAN 1. Why should it hurt? They said it's a natural thing, the most natural thing in all creation. It's happened millions of times already so I guess the procedure has been pretty well refined by now. Look, don't fret about it. They all said it's going to be real nice and—uh—natural. Real —ah—nice.

MAN 2. *(After a pause.)* You know something? It might not be just like they told us.

MAN 1. What gives you that idea? It all sounded pretty authentic to me. You know, we have no reason to question anything.

MAN 2. *(Shrugs.)* Huh. *(Sudden movement startles* w1.)

WOMAN 1. What are you doing?

MAN 2. Do you mind if I stretch?

WOMAN 1. Oh. I thought you were—

MAN 2. Listen. When it happens, you'll know.

WOMAN 1. . . . I wonder how it's going to happen.

MAN 2. What's the use of wondering?

WOMAN 1. Aren't you curious? I can't wait to see what happens.

MAN 2. I can wait.

MAN 1. We have to wait.

WOMAN 1. *(Waxing ecstatic.)* Suppose it's like . . . like an explosion of joy —whatever that is! Or—or maybe it's a total change into a new being, like making an angel out of an animal. Do you think it's like that? Like a magnificent metamorphosis, like a glorious sensation or a grand dream that all of a sudden turns out to be true? . . . I'll bet it's like nothing we've ever experienced.

MAN 2. I'll buy that.

MAN 1. After all, we haven't much of anything to compare it with.

MAN 2. I say it's not worth speculating about. When it comes, it comes, that's all. And it may be distasteful in some way, you know. It might be a bloody mess, as a matter of fact. Then too, it may happen so fast you won't even remember it. *(Makes a whizzing sound.)* Shhhissh! And it's done!

WOMAN 1. You may be right. I mean—we don't know. You're right, why speculate about it. . . . But I'm looking forward to—afterward. It looks so green and cool down there and, well, solid. This isn't bad for a place to wait, but after all, it's not solid.

MAN 2. It's a nice place to wait, but you don't want to stay here.

WOMAN 1. No. Of course, nobody does. *(Noticing that* w2 *is asleep— possibly from the beginning.)* Hey! Look at this one—doesn't she have any curiosity? Low-blood-pressure type! *(Pretending to shake her.)* Hey, you with the eyelids—wake up!

WOMAN 2. *(Startled awake.)* What? Is it time?

WOMAN 1. Time? Nobody knows the meaning of that word here.

WOMAN 2. I mean, is it time to get ready?

WOMAN 1. We're all ready, as far as that goes, and I doubt if there's going to be any warning.

MAN 1. If you're talking about departure time, nobody knows anything but what they told us. You've been to the briefing sessions. You know that we're scheduled for immediate delivery.

WOMAN 1. Whatever that means.

MAN 1. It means soon, I guess. But, as they say, you can't hurry the Boss.

WOMAN 2. *(Stretching or rubbing her eyes.)* Why did you wake me, if it's not time?

WOMAN 1. For heaven's sake! How can you sleep now?

WOMAN 2. I—I don't know. I guess I—I wanted to get away from the tension of waiting. . . . Maybe to retreat . . . draw back from the—the yawning unknown ahead of us.

MAN 2. Scared?

WOMAN 2. Scared? No. No, I'm petrified! Oh—it's not that I don't want to go. I volunteered like the rest of you. But I've had, well, second thoughts—since I made that commitment. It's a rather final step. Well, I don't know that I'm prepared for the experience.

WOMAN 1. None of us is prepared for it, dear. But we have to be ready.

MAN 1. They told us there's no way to prepare for it.

MAN 2. I wouldn't think about it too much in advance, if I were you. (BUTCHER *enters.)* Well, hello!

BUTCHER. Hello.

WOMAN 1. Hi, there.

WOMAN 2. How do you do?

BUTCHER. Geez, that's one question I can't answer right now.

MAN 1. Are you here for us, sir?

BUTCHER. What?

WOMAN 2. *(Eagerly.)* Are you the delivery boy?

BUTCHER. *(Incredulous.)* Lady, I don't think I know what you're talking about! Huh. You must have me confused with Johnny—he used to work for me Saturdays when the old biddies would call up and want their groceries delivered for Sunday. No lady, I'm not the delivery boy. I'm the owner—*(catching himself)* was the owner. Marvin's Meat Market, that's what it was. You follow?

WOMAN 2. *(Disappointed.)* Then—you're not the one to—to get us born?

BUTCHER. Born? Born! *(Laughs loudly.)* Lady, I don't know what fairy tales you got ahold of but—born! Do I look like a stupid stork? . . . Did you really say—born?

MAN 1. Yes, born. I guess you don't understand. You see—

BUTCHER. Oh, yeah, I get it. I think. Then I'm in the wrong room. Unless . . . Oh, no! No, not that! What a helluva deal! They couldn't do that to me, not in a thousand years! *(Wonderingly.)* Could they?

MAN 1. Do what?

BUTCHER. Well, now, you're here waitin' to be born, right? On the other hand, see, I been born. That's right. Born, lived, and died. And now I'm waitin' around for the—ah—final disposition of my case. Which won't take long, friends, as I've hardly got a thing on the merit side on account of I didn't do much for my fellowman. Which means them accountants won't have to puzzle over the books too long. I'm no saint, see? But then, saints don't come along every minute of every day. Like, almost never. If you know what I mean.

MAN 2. But—what are you doing in this room, mister? If you're already dead?

BUTCHER. It's a mistake, I'm tellin' you, a big lousy mistake! You can't trust these clowns to get anything right! Somebody down the hall said wait in the second room on the right—or did he say the seventh room was right—or . . . hell, it's a maze of doors and hallways here! It's ridiculous the way they take care of returnees! That's what they call us, you know. With all these angels they oughta be able to get a guy in the right room, see? . . . Huh. Know anything about the one they call The Boss?

WOMAN 1. Not very much.

BUTCHER. Well, he don't stay on top of things, I'll tell you that.

MAN 2. *(Putting it together slowly.)* If I understand you, mister, you have just died. That's weird. Really weird. You dead, and we're about to be born.

BUTCHER. Yeah. We meet comin' and goin', if you know what I mean.

MAN 2. But why? Why would they allow this encounter?

BUTCHER. I doubt if they meant to, buddy. I just got in the wrong room! At least, I hope that's it! The other possibility—brother! That would be the last straw!

WOMAN 1. What do you mean?

BUTCHER. I hate to mention it, even. *(Speaking more intimately.)* Who knows, the walls may have ears. But—ah—anybody around here ever say anything about—reincarnation?

MAN 1. Oh, no. No.

BUTCHER. None of you—I mean, this is your first time, right?

MAN 1. Right.

WOMAN 1. It certainly is. If we ever get started!

BUTCHER. That's a relief. *(Sighs deeply.)* Look, I'm not gonna go through that again. Life is for the dodo birds. The birds can have it! For humans it's like nothin' I wanta try again. I've had it, see? I was glad to die. Well, not glad exactly, but relieved. Satisfied. And I'm not goin' back there, no matter what! . . . Are you sure you heard nothin' about—

MAN 1. We heard nothing about reincarnation.

WOMAN 2. They promised us life, but they didn't say whether life is singular or plural.

BUTCHER. Singular or plural! *(Laughing.)* That's a good one! *(Now deadly serious.)* Well, it better be singular. It's a singular thing when it makes sense, believe me. It makes sense to a few, just the lucky ones. For the rest of us, the vast majority, it's nonsense—garbage! Huh. *(Assuming a reflective tone.)* When I saw my wife's tears fall on that coffin, I said, "Don't you cry for me, woman. I'm gonna weep for you." Well, there wasn't over half a dozen at the funeral, see? Yeah, I saw it all. *(Sighs.)* Half a dozen. You burn yourself out for fifty-six lousy years and when it's all over nobody cares. Just a few. A handful, they care enough to come in and shake your widow's hand. The rest, they don't even notice when you're gone—not until the prices go up and they see the sign that says Under New Management. *(Coming to himself.)* Look, I hafta get outa here. I ain't supposed to be here, see? Where's the door?

MAN 1. Over there, where you came in.

BUTCHER. Don't get smart, buddy. Hope it's still open. *(He tries the knob.)* Good, now I can get this straightened out. Look people, before I go, I—I'm sorry for this. Sorry about what I said. It wasn't—uh—the right thing to say to you guys. Forget what I said and have fun bein' born. Enjoy! Enjoy! *(Laughs bitterly, then stops abruptly as he sees their* *sober stares.)* Whatsamatter, you don't think it's so funny? Look, what do I know about life? I'm just a neighborhood butcher, a meat grinder. That is—plus the fact that I had to go out and hack to make a living on the side. But I had that store for twenty-six lousy years! Marvin's Meat Market. Sausage and salami, ham and hamburger. Apples, fifty cents a dozen. I never got anywhere in life except to the loan shark. Forget you saw me—what do I know about it? Forget everything!

WOMAN 2. They told us we'll forget what happened before birth. This waiting room and everything.

BUTCHER. Yeah? Well, down below they got another kind of waitin' room. Where the lucky daddy waits and chews his nails wonderin' how to pay off the doctors and the hospital. Huh . . . *(Changing from bitter sarcasm to inquisitiveness.)* You think I came through a waitin' room like this?

MAN 2. They all do.

BUTCHER. Huh. Well, cheers! *(Again sarcastic.)* And watch out for diaper rash! *(Turning as if to leave.)*

WOMAN 1. Wait, mister, don't go yet! *(He turns back.)* I'd like to hear more about—well, earth and life and—everything. We're tired of sitting around here with nothing to do.

BUTCHER. And so you want me to provide some entertainment? No thanks.

WOMAN 1. We want enlightenment. And since we won't remember anyway, what's the harm?

MAN 2. Sure. Describe it for us. You see, they haven't given us much specific information about life.

BUTCHER. No, I don't guess they have.

WOMAN 1. Just that it's a vast wonderful world and we're going to be free to make choices and explore the heights and depths of human existence.

BUTCHER. *(Sarcastically.)* Sure!

MAN 2. I suspect they've been purposely vague. But we volunteered because it sounded good. And we're curious about life, and love, and freedom.

MAN 1. And the Boss ought to know what he's doing.

WOMAN 2. Yes, it sounds solid and exciting—and real!

BUTCHER. Some snow job they gave you! Look, I'll see ya around. There's gonna be a judgment on my case and I better be there. . . . *(Shaking his head sadly.)* Anyway, if you listen to me . . .

WOMAN 1. Yes?

BUTCHER. You're gonna get discouraged.

WOMAN 1. But why?

BUTCHER. Let me ask you this: do you people have any foreknowledge?

WOMAN 1. What?

BUTCHER. You know, the scoop about the future. . . . Somebody mentioned freedom. That's a heap big joke, freedom is! . . . Listen, you are bound forever by the awful accident of birth—where you live and how you live! And it's ten to one you're gonna be poor and miserable, not rich and respectable. That's no choice—that's all settled for you by the accident of birth. . . . *(Sharply.)* What do you know about it?

MAN 1. We have a few details about the circumstances.

BUTCHER. Such as?

MAN 1. Place, parents, a few incidentals.

BUTCHER. Yeah? What's your name, then?

MAN 1. We haven't been named yet.

BUTCHER. I forgot. That's the privilege they save for the parents. So you wind up as Cornelius or Hortense or something. The nerve of parents, taking out their frustrations on their kids like that! Freedom, you say? Free choice? You don't even have a choice of names. Freedom is bull!
. . . *(Addressing* M1.) Well, what are the incidentals, friend?

MAN 1. I am to be born into a good French neighborhood to devoted Christian parents.

BUTCHER. Uh-oh, look out for the churchy ones! Look, it's my experience that the religious parents are the strictest. Don't ever smile because your old man will tan your hide for some imagined sin because he's feeling guilty about his own wild oats. And they are good at tanning hides, those people.

MAN 1. Aren't you generalizing, mister? Are you being fair?

BUTCHER. Okay, so maybe I got carried away. Maybe you'll be lucky. I hope so, pal. Let's just say that I ain't so impressed with the churchy ones. I hope your parents aren't the kind that wear their religion on their sleeves like a sergeant's stripes. . . . *(Now addressing* W2.) What about your situation, sis?

WOMAN 2. I'm going to India. My parents are farmers.

BUTCHER. Oh, no!

WOMAN 2. What's wrong with that, mister? The angel admitted that India's not affluent like the Western nations but it has an ancient and very cultured civilization and the climate isn't bad. Food is scarce now but agricultural innovations are going to revolutionize the country!

BUTCHER. Sez who?

WOMAN 2. The angel implied that the conditions—

BUTCHER. *(Raising his voice.)* Implied, implied! This line they're feeding you is like cotton candy. It tastes sweet but, man, it's all air! India, my dear, is a very backward country where half the people are dying of malnu— mal—anyway, they're hungry and starving. If your parents are peasants you can look forward to a life of sweat and struggle— yeah, struggle to survive! There will be days when your belly is so empty and your throat's so parched you would give anything to be back here biting your fingernails in limbo—that is, if you did remember where you came from.

WOMAN 1. But what makes you an authority on India?

MAN 2. *(Incensed.)* Just because he lived on earth he thinks he knows everything about everything. Just where did you live, anyway?

BUTCHER. West Philly. That means nothing to you, of course. You're right, pal, I don't know a whole lot about India. But I know a whole lot more than any of you clowns know, which, it seems to me, is about zero!

MAN 1. Wherever you lived, sir, it seems to have colored your whole perspective and made you cynical. Now our friend here is to be born in India. That's a decent, respectable country. You've no right to fill her mind full of doubts!

WOMAN 1. *(Half rising in anger.)* No right, no right at all!

BUTCHER. Hold on—just cool it, lady! If I recollect, you're the one wanted me to stay and talk about earth. *(She sinks back, remembering.)* Well, all of you did—it wasn't my idea. If you don't wanna hear no more, if you wanna stay dumb, okay. You prospective thumb-suckers can plop outa your mother's womb fat, dumb, and happy—but you won't stay happy long! Go ahead, see if I care! Somebody said there's a sucker born every minute. Think it was Barnum. You know—Barnum and Bailey Circus? You don't know. . . . All right, forget it. I'm leaving! *(Half turns away.)*

WOMAN 2. Wait. Don't go.

WOMAN 1. I'm sorry I was so rude. Please . . . you haven't told me about America.

BUTCHER. *(Turning back.)* Oh, so you're gonna get born in America.

WOMAN 1. It's a small town in Indiana.

BUTCHER. What kind of parents?

WOMAN 1. Oh—my mother isn't married but—

BUTCHER. Great!

WOMAN 1. I did want so desperately to be born. And she's supposed to be

a fine person. She was so innocent when it happened. She believed
he loved her—

BUTCHER. They all do.

WOMAN 1. And she's going to keep her baby. That's me! She wants to
because she loves children and she wants to have me and make me
happy. Already she loves me. I know it's not the best situation but love
is important, isn't it? And her parents are going to help raise me
because they love their daughter and their unborn grandchild. Isn't
that wonderful? Isn't it grand when you're loved?

BUTCHER. Oh, yeah. It sure is.

WOMAN 1. I'm so glad. I thought it was going to be all right.

BUTCHER. Oh—ah—I wouldn't say that. Not really.

WOMAN 1. What do you mean?

MAN 2. Here it comes.

WOMAN 2. Don't listen to him, dear.

MAN 2. Look, he hasn't shown us his credentials or anything. We don't
know this man!

WOMAN 1. I want to know about earth! You people can all shut your ears
but I want to know!

BUTCHER. Sure you do. And I wish I could reassure you and feed you the
line, "Love is all that matters." But I can't. A lotta things matter.
Listen, love won't erase that girl's memories. Your mother, I mean.
You say she's nice and all that.

WOMAN 1. That's what the report said.

BUTCHER. Then she's got a helluva conscience. Nice girls do. That means
every time she looks at you she's feelin' guilty about the sex that got
you started. You do know about sex, don't you? Well, she's gonna hate
herself for it—yeah, and you're the symbol of that guilt so she's gonna
hate you for it too! (*More and more disturbed by his description,* w1
now breaks into sobs.) That's too bad for you, poor kid . . . (*After a
moment, not unkindly.*) Anybody else want me to tell his fortune?

MAN 2. Well, I'm—I'm going to South Africa.

BUTCHER. White parents, I hope? (M2 *shakes his head no.*) Tough! Well,
you can always hope for a miracle like a miscarriage. But I guess it's
too late for that, eh? Huh. Better to be born into the Philadelphia
ghetto with an absentee father than in South Africa with all that apar
— apartheid. Look, my advice to all of you is to cop out on this trip
—get out of here! They were right that hell is down—it's down there
on planet earth, that madly spinning world. It's a mad world full of
stubborn selfish animals who won't give a spit for you unless you can
do something for them.

MAN 1. What do you mean?

BUTCHER. The world's full of two kinds of people: snobs and slobs. The snobs think they're better than you; the slobs don't care. They don't care about you and they don't care about nothin'! The snobs like to keep you on the rug where they can walk on you; the slobs don't even let on that you exist.

MAN 2. Is it that bad?

BUTCHER. You can't be a person down there. Did I have to struggle in the meat business! Finally I gave it up because I couldn't stand any more suspicious housewives snooping around to see whether I doctored the hamburger to make it look red. The hell of it is I had to do it to stay in business—otherwise you have to throw out half your meat some nights. With a small store you can't afford that. . . . And if you think I had problems in Philly, look at Africa or India or South America. Earth is crowded with sad-eyed, drooping, miserable people nobody cares about. Nobody's gettin' any love unless he's one of the lucky three percent. (*Now to* M1.) Where's your birthplace gonna be?

MAN 1. I don't think I'll tell you.

BUTCHER. That's your business. But it looks like what I've said's disturbed you.

MAN 1. Well, naturally . . .

MAN 2. Sure, it's disturbing.

WOMAN 2. I'm very surprised.

MAN 1. Why should we listen to this man?

WOMAN 1. I'm glad he came. We needed to know these things.

WOMAN 2. I don't like the picture he's painting, not at all.

BUTCHER. It's a lulu—but it's straight, believe me.

MAN 2. If what you say is true . . .

BUTCHER. Can you cop out?

MAN 1. Cop—out?

BUTCHER. Yeah, can't you refuse your assignment?

MAN 1. Well, I suppose that is possible. But nobody has ever done so, as far as we know. I mean, once committed . . .

BUTCHER. Well, if I were you I wouldn't stand for it. No, sir! You thumb-suckers oughta rebel 'fore it's too late. When you're in the nursery, you know, you can't stand up in the crib and say "I wanna go back!" Listen—if somebody had given me this scoop when I was in this waitin' room I would've . . .

MAN 1. Sure!

WOMAN 1. What would you have done, mister?

BUTCHER. Well, I guess I . . . *(Thinking hard.)* I woulda revolted! We could stage a demonstration against this inhuman system that makes you slaves in a hostile environment! What are you anyhow, men or mice?

MAN 2. We're nothing yet.

BUTCHER. Yeah, and there's the awful accident of birth. You could be born mice and it won't make no difference 'cause you won't be men anyway. Lots of people down there live like rats! Boy, the neighborhood sure changed since I was a kid. Right now there's three families living in the third-floor apartment in my building—with a toilet that don't work 'cause the lousy water pressure's too low!

WOMAN 2. Three families?

BUTCHER. In a small flat about twice the size of this waitin' room. Sure I complained but the owner never did nothing—cost too much to fix it up. . . . But suppose you are lucky. *(Addressing w1.)* Suppose that girl does love you and suppose you grow up in that Hoosier village. Okay, what've you got to look forward to? A world of pain and pomp and prejudice—tension, tension, always tension—and the inevitable wars that get bigger and more explosive all the time. You know they've got a poison gas now that's so powerful it'd take one cubic inch of it to poison a whole nation? And do you know what they're fixin' to do right now? Do you? They've got rockets that can blow up the globe twenty times over! How does that sound to you nuts who are about to become cuddly little bundles of babyhood? *(With mock salute.)* I salute you who are about to be born: you are either very, very brave or very, very stupid.

The others react anxiously, speak in tense tones.

WOMAN 2. He's giving me the creeps!

WOMAN 1. Maybe he's right, though.

MAN 2. Sure. We ought to protest. The system isn't fair—I always thought that!

MAN 1. Even if he is right, what can we do?

WOMAN 1. We should march on the palace and demand our rights!

MAN 1. What rights?

WOMAN 2. What palace?

WOMAN 1. The recruiting angel said the Boss lives in a palace.

MAN 1. My angel said he doesn't live anywhere.

BUTCHER. They oughta get their stories straight.

WOMAN 1. Never mind that. Let's get up some sort of protest. They ought to hear our grievances! Let's petition the administration, demand reform! *(Addressing BUTCHER.)* Will you help us, mister?

BUTCHER. Sure. *(Rising in place.)* First you need some snappy slogans.

We can put 'em on placards, see? Some key words, cute phrases that'll bring your complaints immediately to their eyes. Slogans like—ah— "Freedom Now!"

MAN 1. *(Puzzled.)* Freedom—now?

BUTCHER. Yeah. Well, it's selling good down below. . . . How about "Shame!"

MAN 1. Shame?

BUTCHER. Appropriate to every situation, see? A good shame sign can be used over and over. Very durable. Now here's one for you: "No Conception Without Representation."

WOMAN 1. I like that. *(Rising in place.)* And how about this: "We Demand the Right to Choose Our Views!"

BUTCHER. That's real catchy. Any others?

WOMAN 2. *(Rising.)* "Guaranteed Respectability!"

BUTCHER. Fine.

MAN 2. *(Rising.)* "Illegitimate Births Are Not Humane!"

MAN 1. *(Rising.)* "We Won't Be Born into Substandard Neighborhoods!"

WOMAN 2. "Make Minimum Living Standards Mandatory!"

WOMAN 1. "We Who Are About to Be Born Salute No One!"

MAN 1. "Guaranteed Comfort!"

MAN 2. "Guaranteed Personhood!"

WOMAN 2. "Live, Not Exist!"

BUTCHER. That's swell, now you're catching on! If you organize into a union, see, you can do some collective bargaining with the Boss and beat the system! Demand a contract that has all you want from life, and no problems. Now let's get a good rhyme and we'll learn to sing it. That always gets 'em . . . *(Thinking hard.)* How 'bout . . . "We are the salt of the earth . . ."

WOMAN 1. "And . . . we want the freedom of birth!"

BUTCHER. Good, good. Second line?

WOMAN 2. "We aren't going to be . . . foundlings . . . we want nice surroundings . . ."

WOMAN 1. "We're not things; we are . . . people of worth!"

BUTCHER. Great! Let's sing it out now!

(They begin to chant this refrain together, with the BUTCHER acting as a kind of cheerleader. They chant the refrain twice, getting more spirited as it develops. By the end they are shouting boisterously. The second time they should begin to march in place, suggesting a prancing, moving, protest demonstration. Everything builds to the climax: the entrance of the ANGEL.)

Together, twice through:
    "We are the salt of the earth,
    And we want the freedom of birth!
    We aren't going to be foundlings; we want nice surroundings—
    We're not things; we are people of worth!"

(The ANGEL *enters, standing. All except the* BUTCHER *embarrassedly sit down, staggered fashion. Dead silence for a moment.)*

ANGEL. What's going on here?

BUTCHER. . . . Ah—nothing, Angel. . . . Just a—just a harmless little demon-stration.

ANGEL. *(Sharply.)* Not permitted!

BUTCHER. Who says?

ANGEL. *(Firmly.)* The Boss wouldn't like it.

BUTCHER. That's the trouble with this place—the Boss has too much power. I'd like to see that Boss sometime, if he's here at all. Maybe you guys have invented him, for all I know. Maybe the Boss is some kind of imaginary despot you people have invented to keep us in our place.

ANGEL. The Boss is not imaginary, and hardly despotic!

BUTCHER. Yeah? Well, he's got too much authority around here. The Boss don't like this, the Boss don't allow that! Sounds like those thugs from the local syndicate came to see me about payin' off a loan. Well, how 'bout a little democracy here? A little freedom? Well, the point of this little march is to make it clear to you clowns that—

ANGEL. What are you doing here, anyway? This is the wrong room—this is Prenatal!

BUTCHER. Oh, yeah? *(Faking surprise.)* I'll be darned—I must of got in the wrong room by mistake.

ANGEL. Come on now, out you go. *(Pretending to shove him.)* Come on now, move!

BUTCHER. *(Shaking her off.)* I'm not ready yet; the party's just beginnin'. *(As she continues to force his exit.)* Well, okay, if you insist! *(To others.)* You're my witnesses, they're usin' force and coercion here. Police brutality—that's what it is! *(Exits.)* You're my witnesses!

ANGEL. *(Wiping her brow.)* Whew! There's a strange one. I don't know what he's been telling you . . .

WOMAN 1. He's been telling us terrible things about life, like how painful it's going to be and—

ANGEL. So that's it! *(Sinking onto her stool.)* O Lord, I knew this would happen! My goodness, if the Boss finds out about this! *(Flustered, perhaps waving her handkerchief.)* We've tried to keep everybody separate! I was afraid that if one of them got into this waiting room— Well, these returnees are nice people—most of them. Some of them are saints and lots of them get honors and awards and nice suites up in the mansion. But others—well, this one for instance. He probably told you that the earth is full of wickedness et cetera.

MAN 1. He did, yes.

ANGEL. Sad case. Sad, sad case. We try to send everyone into life full of hope and expectancy, because it can be beautiful if you want it to be. But some of them—well, they get corrupted despite our precautions. We're not allowed to brainwash people, you know—just make suggestions. It's a mystery to me how they get corrupted so easily, some of them. I really can't understand it because I've never lived on earth myself. Of course, we have our sources of information. . . . Oh, my goodness, I hope you didn't listen to that fellow. He's certainly not a good representative.

WOMAN 1. Some of us thought he was rather convincing.

MAN 1. He did seem to know what he was talking about.

ANGEL. Oh, no! What's the Boss going to say? Good grief! I could lose my wings for this and that's no fun for an angel!

WOMAN 2. He said that earth is full of sordid things and selfish people and wars and famine and—

ANGEL. *(Quite disturbed.)* He is sick! How could earth be so bad? The Boss established the whole business, you know. Well, none of us angels get down to earth much but—

MAN 1. I thought there were guardian angels.

ANGEL. In a sense, yes. But you're really on your own down there. Basically you make your own decisions. That's the great thing about life —the chance to choose.

MAN 2. So we heard.

MAN 1. That man said that choice is an illusion.

ANGEL. That's a two-bit cynic talking. Don't you believe it! The one thing nobody can take from you is the power to develop an attitude, chart your own course, make something real from what is given you.

WOMAN 1. But was the Butcher right? Is there such dreadful suffering on earth? Is there a loneliness so terrible we can hardly stand it?

ANGEL. Now please don't fret about such things. Really, that man! We're going to have to do something about locks for these doors!

WOMAN 1. *(Insistent.)* Please answer my question.

ANGEL. *(Sighs deeply, shakes her head.)* Frankly, I don't have all the answers. I just work here. Pain? Some perhaps, but nothing you cannot endure. I'm sure of that.

WOMAN 1. But why should there be pain?

ANGEL. Don't expect any final answer to that one, dear.

WOMAN 1. Why not?

ANGEL. At least there's no answer on earth. Not until your minds are put on the stretching-racks of heaven can you begin to follow the whys and wherefores of this universe. Go into life asking your questions. Yell out your "How come?" whenever you want. But you may have to be content with the smallest clues to an answer. That's the way life is, I'm told. A glorious mystery. A hero trip through the unknowable, not an excursion but an expedition. Pain will bring out the best that is in you . . . or the worst. . . . The Boss is willing to take the gamble.

MAN 2. But . . . if we decide . . . That is—do we still have a choice?

WOMAN 1. Can we still say no to birth?

ANGEL. *(Perplexed.)* It's never . . . it's rather late for that, you know. . . . Still—the Boss said long ago that it has to be voluntary. Nobody has to go. But, please, consider it carefully. If you miss it this time your names go to the bottom of the list, and it will take a long time before . . . *(Nervously preparing to leave.)* Uh-oh, I'd better go chase that Butcher. If I don't keep track of him they might take away my halo! Cheer up, the worst has never been. *(With a cheery wave.)* Ta-ta! *(Exits.)*

MAN 2. *(A long thoughtful pause. Then, irately.)* I'm getting out of here! What about the rest of you?

WOMAN 1. I don't know.

MAN 2. You don't know, you don't know! Did you let that angel brainwash you again?

WOMAN 1. I did want to be born.

MAN 2. *(Disgusted.)* Aaah!

WOMAN 1. It looked so beautiful in the brochures. *(Waxing ecstatic again.)* The chance to have a family, to enjoy affection, to sit in the soft spring air and hear the sounds of the earth, to feel the dew against your face, to touch the happy smile of a child, to participate, to be alive—it sounded and it looked so marvelous! And despite what that man said,

I can't really believe it's so bad. When that angel talks about life, it sounds so good.

WOMAN 2. It must be good. Just to be alive, to have a real existence. To taste and touch, to hear and be heard, to love and be loved, to work and play and to see things grow and to feel yourself growing and to help others to grow. Isn't that what life is all about?

MAN 1. Here we're just—hanging—just being. We're not becoming anything. Life is development, life must be a becoming.

MAN 2. Well, I don't buy that soft stuff! You're all dupes of the system here! All the information we get is controlled, carefully managed, and sifted, so that we learn just what they want us to learn about life.

MAN 1. *(Angered.)* You have no proof of that!

MAN 2. And you can't deny it either! Now for once we hear from somebody who's not controlled, who gives us the straight talk they don't want us to hear! That's right! The Butcher! Didn't you listen to him? He's been there, he's seen it, he knows what it's like! And you—you uncritically take the word of an angel who's never lived on earth! All she knows is what the Boss tells her to tell us. How do we know that's the truth?

MAN 1. We don't know.

MAN 2. That's right, we don't.

MAN 1. But that's the whole idea, isn't it? We have to dare to believe because that itself is the first step. Look, if you want a guarantee or something, you're not going to get it. . . . *(Thoughtfully.)* I know this much. I'm not going to pass it up and then kick myself from here to eternity. I'm going to accept that dare. I gather that most of you feel as I do. . . . Sure, it's a gamble. But you have to trust the Boss.

MAN 2. Why?

MAN 1. Because he's the Boss, that's why. And because he's fair.

MAN 2. Is he?

MAN 1. Sure.

MAN 2. How do you know that?

MAN 1. It's part of his nature. He's solid and he's true.

MAN 2. So they say. But if this weird world of his is half as brutal and chaotic as that man described it . . .

MAN 1. That's not possible. If the Boss is really in charge . . . *(Long pause. Shifting uncomfortably.)* Anyway . . . we have to trust him.

MAN 2. *(Vehemently.)* Why?

MAN 1. There's nobody else to trust.

Finding Literature: A Suggestive Listing

Without any pretense of being comprehensive, I present a fragmentary listing of literature which is religiously profound and which may prove to be, at least in part, adaptable for group reading in the church. This should trigger additional ideas in those who know their literature better than I do.

Short Stories

There are many Christmas stories that adapt well, such as Dickens' immortal *A Christmas Carol* and Henry van Dyke's *The Story of the Other Wise Man*. O. Henry's "The Gift of the Magi" is included here. Also check the compiled program "Christmas Comes but Once a Year" for ideas.

There are some classic short stories that would work, such as Stephen Vincent Benét's "The Devil and Daniel Webster." Look through the anthologies; the best one for your purposes could be *The Questing Spirit: Religion in the Literature of Our Time*, edited by Halford E. Luccock and Frances Brentano (New York: Coward-McCann, 1947). Several stories in *The Innovator and Other Modern Parables*, by G. William Jones (Nashville: Abingdon Press, 1962), would make exciting reading.

And don't forget children's stories! Many of them are humorous, thought-generating, and pleasantly moralistic. Examine the old classics like *Alice in Wonderland* and "The Emperor's New Clothes" for their religious values, and utilize some of the fine modern children's tales, like *The Cookie Tree* by Jay Williams (New York: Parents Magazine Press, 1967), which convey Christian ideals or moral principles. Sometimes fables and stories from other lands, like India or Mexico, are useful. And don't overlook old Aesop as a source of sermon starters!

Novels

Countless novels contain material of religious significance, from *Cry, the Beloved Country* to *To Sir, With Love*. Pieces of old classics like *Les Misérables* can be resurrected. Don't overlook some of the very earthy, even profane modern writing which may contain insight into the human condition and which may dramatize man's values and his spiritual needs. As one example, consider Salinger's *Franny and Zooey;* if you can get by the profanity you'll find some interesting dialogue, even one offbeat episode which is strangely incarnational theology. Other possibilities:

Adela Rogers St. Johns, *Tell No Man.* The exciting, upsetting story of a businessman-turned-preacher who is determined to take Jesus' promises seriously and to act on them. Has several very readable and lively scenes.

Ray Bradbury, *Dandelion Wine.* Celebration of life as seen through the eyes of a young boy enjoying a small-town summer. Unusual incidental study of the meaning of death as seen through his mind's eye. Coger and White include an adaptation of this novel in their *Readers Theatre Handbook.*

Lloyd C. Douglas, *The Robe* and *The Big Fisherman.* These popular Biblical novels make excellent reading. Others include Taylor Caldwell, *Great Lion of God;* Thomas B. Costain, *The Silver Chalice;* and Lew Wallace, *Ben Hur.*

Biographies

Biographies and autobiographies of Christian heroes (Schweitzer, Lincoln, Niemoeller, Bonhoeffer, Martin Luther King, Jr., etc.) often have dramatic qualities; certain scenes, at least, may become Readers Theatre. Biographies by other than Christian heroes (for example, Mark Twain) may be instructive in part.

Columns and Essays

Many writings of columnists are humorous, others are profound, and some are both (witness the Al Martinez piece in this book). Often their work is not obviously religious, but may have a message in it. Such writers as Art Buchwald, Arthur Hoppe, Russell Baker, and Sandy Grady often write in dialogue form, which makes their work quite adaptable. Remember, great sermons can be preached satirically, as these authors prove.

Poetry

These poems have been done effectively as Readers Theatre:
W. H. Auden, *For the Time Being; The Age of Anxiety*
Robert Frost, "The Death of the Hired Man"
Hermann Hagedorn, *The Bomb That Fell on America*
Amy Lowell, "The Day That Was That Day"
John Masefield, *Enslaved*
Edgar Lee Masters, *Spoon River Anthology*
Dylan Thomas, *Under Milk Wood*

The poem by Amy Lowell may be found in the Coger-White manual. Remember that most poetry is difficult to adapt since it tends to be highly abstract and is written in but one voice. Look for poetry with a narrative line and several voices or characters.

Full-Length Plays

Remember, you don't have to do the entire play! These plays all have significant scenes that might be cut or edited for reading in worship or in other church endeavors:

Maxwell Anderson, *Joan of Lorraine*
Jean Anouilh, *Becket*; *The Lark*
Robert Bolt, *A Man for All Seasons*
Marc Connelly, *The Green Pastures*
Louis O. Coxe and Robert Chapman, Melville's *Billy Budd*
Friedrich Duerrenmatt, *The Visit*
T. S. Eliot, *Murder in the Cathedral*; *The Cocktail Party*
Lorraine Hansberry, *A Raisin in the Sun*
Rolf Hochhuth, *The Deputy*
Eugène Ionesco, *Rhinoceros*
Archibald MacLeish, *J.B.*; *Scratch*
Christopher Marlowe, *The Tragedy of Dr. Faustus*
John Masefield, *The Trial of Jesus*
Arthur Miller, *Death of a Salesman*; *Incident at Vichy*;
     All My Sons; *The Crucible*
N. Richard Nash, *The Rainmaker*
John Osborne, *Luther*
Dorothy Sayers, *The Man Born to Be King*
William Shakespeare, *Macbeth*; *Hamlet*; etc.
George Bernard Shaw, *Androcles and the Lion*; *Saint Joan*
Sophocles, *Antigone*
Thornton Wilder, *Our Town*; *The Skin of Our Teeth*

One-Acts

One-act plays may not require as much editing as full-length plays. The following are one-acts I find particularly useful as a Christian dramatist; they are possibilities for reading!

Stephen Vincent Benét, *A Child Is Born*
Albert Johnson, *Roger Williams and Mary*
Charles Rann Kennedy, *The Terrible Meek*
Pär Lagerkvist, *Let Man Live*
William Saroyan, *Coming Through the Rye*
Ralph Stone, *Construction*
Philip William Turner, *Christ in the Concrete City*
R. H. Ward, *The Holy Family*; *The Figure on the Cross*

Norman Dietz has a collection, *Fables & Vaudevilles & Plays* (John Knox Press, 1968), which includes some delightful two- and three-character dramatic bits written with lots of offbeat Christian humor—such titles as *The Apple Bit, Harry and the Angel,* and *Old Ymir's Clay Pot*. I have used *Old Ymir* as the dramatic sermon in three worship experiences.

Another interesting assortment of Christian one-acts is by Henri Gheon and H. Brochet, *St. Anne and the Gouty Rector, and Other Plays* (New York: David McKay Co., 1950). *The Gardener Who Was Afraid of Death* is my favorite.

What about theatre of the absurd, which is largely one-acts? Certain plays of this genre, while not written from a Christian world view, still make good reading and help us understand the human condition. Examine Ionesco's *The Bald Soprano* for the theme of man's failure to communicate and *The Chairs* as a study in futility. Albee's *The Zoo Story* is an illustration of man's desperate groping for meaningful relationship. Many other plays of this type are too visual, not verbal enough, to read well— and many others are too gross or opaque to be used in a church setting.

I have written several one-acts that might adapt for Readers Theatre, aside from *The Waiting Room*, which is included. Others are the following:

God Is My Fuehrer (New York: Friendship Press, 1970), $1.50. Nonroyalty. The life and times of Dr. Martin Niemoeller, the German pastor who dared to oppose the Nazis. Easy to adapt for reading since it includes narration. Sound effects suggested. Entire play can be read by three men, two women.

The Way Station, 4 men, 2 women. A modern morality play in which the afterlife is a device for commentary on this life; it treats interpersonal relationships. Five dead people find themselves in a hazy limbo and look for a way to reach the distant "palace." Could be staged with reading stands and candles.

On the Plain of Dura, 3m, 1w, or more. A choric drama based on the story in Daniel 3 and relating to contemporary "golden images" of pleasure, possessions, power. Choric sections interweave dramatic scenes in the mythical court of King Nebuchadnezzar.

From Philo, With Love, 6m. A fantasy in three brief scenes. Aliens from distant planet Philo confront the leaders of a small earth village. Disturbed by the invaders' talk of a "Sovereign" who has sent them on a mission of cosmic revolution, the earthmen are hostile, communication breaks down, tragedy occurs; then we discover that the aliens' mission was more spiritual than political. Effective Readers Theatre is possible using two levels and offstage focus, adding some narrative perhaps.

Were You There? (published in the *Baptist Leader*, March 1965). Requires a narrator, three "speakers" (two men, one woman), a speaking chorus of at least four readers, and someone to sing verses of the spiritual "Were You There When They Crucified My Lord?" Good for Lenten or Easter reading. Fictional contemporaries of Jesus retell the story of his death and rising.

For copies of the four preceding plays, write Gordon C. Bennett, 1743 Russell Road, Paoli, Pa. 19301. Single copies are $1.00 plus postage.

A Topical Listing: "Death"

This book does not include a topical listing of materials for Readers Theatre under such headings as "Faith," "Love," "Missions," "Forgiveness." I leave that to others more enterprising. However, to illustrate the variety and diversity of materials which might relate to a particular theme, let's take the general topic of "Death." These materials are all possibilities for that topic:

> Loneliness of death without faith: Ionesco, *Exit the King*; Albee, *The Sandbox*; Miller, *Death of a Salesman*.
>
> Sweet-sadness of death (love lives on!): Dietz, *O To Be Living, O To Be Dying*.
>
> Christian struggling for courage in the face of death: Brochet, *The Gardener Who Was Afraid of Death*.
>
> Christian showing bravery in martyrdom: Shaw, *Saint Joan*; Eliot, *Murder in the Cathedral*; Bolt, *A Man for All Seasons*.
>
> Reacting with faith and courage to death of a loved one: Bennett, *God Is My Fuehrer* (prison scene); Coretta King, *My Life with Martin Luther King, Jr.*; Catherine Marshall, *To Live Again*.
>
> Death as the door to a better world: Lewis, *The Great Divorce*; Bennett, *The Way Station*. To a worse world: Sartre, *No Exit*.
>
> Importance of preparing for death: Medieval play *Everyman*; Jesus' parable of Dives and Lazarus.
>
> Reactions to the death of Jesus: Masefield, *The Trial of Jesus*; Mueller, *Eyes upon the Cross*; Bennett, *Were You There?*

This is a limited sampling of adaptable materials from literature related to the topic of death. Extensive lists of this kind can be developed for any significant theme.

COMPOSITE PROGRAMS

To illustrate how you can arrange a program of readings on a given theme, consider the following programs which were compiled and directed by Dr. Melvin R. White of California State College, Hayward, and presented at Ford Ord, December 11 and 12, 1971.

Americana—From the Printed Page

Material will be chosen from the following:

> "California Essays," Anonymous
>
> "Adam and Eve, Ltd.," an ecological fable by W. B. Park
>
> "The Macbeth Murder Mystery," a short story by James Thurber
>
> "Stamp Out Sex Practices," by Art Hoppe
>
> "Babies Are a Lot of Garbage," by Art Hoppe
>
> "Oh, It All Rings So True to Life, Arthur," by Israel Horowitz

Excerpts from "Americana 1971," including:
    Brickman, "The Small Society"
    Russell Baker, "A Day in the Lives"
    Ernie Hines, "Intergenerational Noncommunication"
    Arnold M. Auerbach, "Love Finds Andy Hardy"
    Al Martinez, "Uncle Sam Wants Who?"
    Art Buchwald, "The Consumer Conspiracy"
    Russell Baker, "All Up in the Air"
    Art Buchwald, "What Is It, Mrs. Perkins?"
    "Passionella," a short story by Jules Feiffer

Christmas Comes but Once a Year

The Past . . .
    St. Luke 2:1–20
    "The Shepherd Who Would Not Go," by Heywood Broun
    Massachusetts Statute, 1660

The Present . . .
    "The Second Shepherd," by Albert Howard Carter
    "Christmas Card Quandary," from "Merry Christmas Plus Peace on
        Earth," by Art Buchwald
    "The Founding of a Business Miracle" and "A Christmas Story" by
        Russell Baker
    "How Mrs. Santa Claus Saved Christmas," by Phyllis McGinley
    "The Errors of Santa Claus," by Stephen Leacock
    "The Twelve Mistakes of Christmas, Not Including That Partridge in
        the Pear Tree," by Ogden Nash

The Future . . .
    "The Gift," by Ray Bradbury

And . . .
    Excerpts from "The Hope of the World," by Robert Quillen

A Brief Bibliography of Reference Works

On Readers Theatre

Coger, Leslie Irene, and White, Melvin R. *Readers Theatre Handbook: A Dramatic Approach to Literature.* Glenview, Ill.: Scott, Foresman and Co., 1967. A revised edition is in preparation.

Maclay, Joanna. *Readers Theatre: Toward a Grammar of Practice.* New York: Random House, 1970.

On Oral Interpretation of Literature

Aggertt, Otis J., and Bowen, Elbert R. *Communicative Reading.* New York: The Macmillan Co., 1963. Excellent textbook.

Armstrong, Chloe. *The Oral Interpretation of Biblical Literature.* Minneapolis: Burgess Publishing Co., 1968. Strong on the analysis and preparation of Biblical materials for solo reading.

Bacon, Wallace A. *The Art of Interpretation.* New York: Holt, Rinehart and Winston, 1966.

Lamar, Nedra Newkirk. *How to Speak the Written Word.* Westwood, N.J.: Fleming H. Revell Co., 1967. Very strong on guidelines for phrasing and stress; deals heavily with the oral reading of Biblical materials.

Lee, Charlotte I. *Oral Interpretation.* Boston: Houghton Mifflin Co., 1965. Good text but rather technical in its discussion of literature.

On Using Drama in the Church

Brandt, Alvin G. *Drama Handbook for Churches.* New York: Seabury Press, 1964.

Ehrensperger, Harold. *Religious Drama: Ends and Means.* Nashville: Abingdon Press, 1962.

Johnson, Albert. *Church Plays and How to Stage Them.* Philadelphia: United Church Press, 1966.

Moseley, J. Edward. *Using Drama in the Church.* St. Louis: Bethany Press, 1955.

Important Lists of Religious Drama

Plays for the Church. National Council of Churches of Christ in the U.S.A., 475 Riverside Drive, New York, N.Y. 10027. A selective listing of the

very best. $1.00. Also, request catalogue of Friendship Press dramas
from the same address.

Albert Johnson, *Best Church Plays: A Bibliography of Religious Drama.*
Philadelphia: Pilgrim Press, 1968. More comprehensive and less dis-
criminating. $3.95.

Catalogue of Religious Plays. Walter H. Baker Co., 100 Summer Street,
Boston, Mass. 02110. Lists all the plays that Baker owns; cannot be
relied upon for objectivity.

(Prices are subject to change.)

Notes

Readers Theatre: Descriptions and Definitions

1. James H. Warren, "The Power of Something Inward: Informal Drama in the Church," *International Journal of Religious Education*, Vol. 37, No. 6 (February 1961), p. 14.
2. Chloe Armstrong and Paul D. Brandes, *The Oral Interpretation of Literature* (New York: McGraw-Hill Book Co., 1963), p. 289.
3. Keith Brooks, "Readers Theatre: Some Questions and Answers," *Dramatics*, Vol. XXXIV, No. 3 (December 1962), p. 14.
4. Wallace A. Bacon, *The Art of Interpretation* (New York: Holt, Rinehart and Winston, 1966), p. 311.
5. Leslie Irene Coger and Melvin R. White, *Readers Theatre Handbook: A Dramatic Approach to Literature* (Glenview, Ill.: Scott, Foresman and Co., 1967), p. 10.
6. *Ibid.*, p. 9.
7. Bacon, *op. cit.*, p. 313.
8. Eugene Bahn and Margaret L. Bahn, *A History of Oral Interpretation* (Minneapolis: Burgess Publishing Co., 1970), chapter 1.
9. Gilbert Austin, *Chironomia* (London, 1806), pp. 203–204.
10. Ann Billups, *Discussion Starters for Youth Groups*, Series One and Series Two (Valley Forge, Pa.: Judson Press, 1966 and 1969).
11. Ronald E. Sleeth, *Persuasive Preaching* (New York: Harper & Brothers, 1956), pp. 77, 66.
12. See the collection by Oscar J. Rumpf, *Cries from the Hurting Edges of the World* (Richmond: John Knox Press, 1970).
13. Warren, *op. cit.*, p. 14.

Finding and Preparing Materials

1. C. S. Lewis, *The Great Divorce* (New York: The Macmillan Co., 1946), p. 27.
2. Norman D. Dietz, *Fables & Vaudevilles & Plays* (Richmond: John Knox Press, 1968), pp. 129–130.
3. William B. McCoard, "Report on the Reading of *Hiroshima*," *Quarterly Journal of Speech*, Vol. 34 (April 1948), pp. 174–175. Used by permission.
4. Gordon C. Bennett, *On the Plain of Dura*, unpublished choric drama. Copyright © 1970 by Gordon C. Bennett.
5. Coger and White, *op. cit.*, p. 34.

Developing Capable Interpreters

1. Paul Hunsinger, *Communicative Interpretation* (Dubuque, Iowa: Wm. C. Brown Co., 1967), pp. 7–9.
2. Luke 1:1–4.

3.   Doris Young, from an unpublished report submitted during the course of Speech 202 at Eastern Baptist College, spring 1970.
4.   Sara Lowrey and Gertrude E. Johnson, *Interpretative Reading* (New York: Appleton-Century-Crofts, 1953), p. 30.
5.   Luke 2:16.
6.   Matthew 20:29.
7.   Ezekiel 18:2.
8.   Luke 9:23.
9.   Bennett, *op. cit.*
10. Coger and White, *op. cit.*, p. 64.

Staging Readers Theatre

1.   In the collection of plays by Ralph Stone, *Circus, Parable, and Construction* (St. Louis: Bethany Press, 1961).
2.   Full-text adaptation for Readers Theatre is included in Coger and White, *op. cit.*
3.   Norman Habel, ed., *What Are We Going to Do with All These Rotting Fish?* (Philadelphia: Fortress Press, 1970).
4.   Coger and White, *op. cit.*, pp. 119–120.